FOREWORD
BISHOP WALTER SCOTT THOMAS

ignite

50 days of prayer
that will CHANGE your life

MATTHEW L. WATLEY

Cover Design: Christoper Thomas of Chris Thomas Graphics
Interior Design: Brandi K. Etheredge
Copy Editor: Yvette R. Blair-Lavallais

TABLE OF CONTENTS

FORWARD

My good friend Matthew Watley provides for us in this book more than inspirational thoughts. He imparts to us the deep spiritual wisdom which causes our hearts to soar in prayer. As you read and pray daily, you will become aware that you are growing stronger spiritually. Perhaps you will notice how your prayers are becoming more focused or how the word of God is becoming more integrated within your prayer life. What I know is that your life will not be the same because your prayer life will be transformed over the next fifty days.

From a pastoral standpoint, one of the reasons that we are sharing this devotional with our congregation is that it is steeped in scripture. It says much about the state of current Christian trends and teachings that a devotional rooted in scripture may be considered unique. Unfortunately, much of what purports itself to be Christian teaching is really only inspirational writing at best. Social media like Facebook and Twitter provide us with more than enough inspirational thoughts. We need a deeper well.

As believers, we must never stray from the central importance of the word of God, which serves as our spiritual guide for knowing the mind of God. Our church, like yours I suspect, is very busy attending to the various needs of our congregation and community. In doing so, it is easy for us to lose our collective strength and Kingdom-focus while we are deployed across various areas of ministry. I have found that one of my most important functions is to call membership together, so that as the body of believers, we can concentrate on larger opportunities that are before us.

As a Christian, there is nothing else that is so personal and powerful that transforms my soul like the power of prayer. Prayer is a course from which no disciple of the Lord Jesus Christ ever graduates. The genius of this book is that by being rooted in the word of God, it serves both the new believer and the seasoned saint equally well. Those who are new to the faith are given a systematic approach to understanding how we ought to pray and how prayer works to transform our lives. For those who have been saved for years, we are given key insights that provide rich, spiritual food and water for hungry souls and parched spirits. The pages that follow are a grand recipe for giving the reader the ingredients and instructions necessary to create spiritual food so that our souls may feast. These pages contain fresh springs of revelation that will ignite a passion for God through a passion of prayer.

Over the course of the next fifty days as you pray, life will continue to happen to you. Life will cause challenges and triumphs to arrive at your doorstep without warning as they always have. What will be different, though, is that as you go to the door to meet them, you will do so in a very different manner. Your prayer life will allow you greater poise and perspective. Life will still impact you and affect you, but now you will also be able to recognize greater opportunities for you to impact and effect your life. Over the next fifty days your eyes will be opened, your heart will be strengthened and your soul will be ignited so that your new prayer life will lead you to live a new and more abundant life.

Bishop Walter Scott Thomas
Senior Pastor, New Psalmist Baptist Church, Baltimore, MD

In Honor

To Rev. Matthew A. Watley and Dr. Lawrence E. Lewis, the men whose names I carry and whose legacies I have sought to keep inviolate all of my life.

Dedication

I wrote this book by the inspiration of the Holy Spirit and at the insistence of my loving wife, Shawna, who has always encouraged me to go beyond my comfort zone. I am grateful to you for seeing more in me than I sometimes see in myself. I dedicate this book to you, dear. I love you and thank God for you daily. And to our daughter, Alexandra Elizabeth (Ally), who is the greatest answer to any prayer that we have ever offered. Mommy and Daddy love you so much!

Acknowledgments

I am indebted to God for all those who have given so generously of their time and energies to making this book possible. To my production team Carolyn Scavella, Yvette Blair-Lavallais, and Brandi Etheredge for making brick without straw, and especially Russell St. Bernard for being clutch twenty-four seven! To Bishop Walter Scott Thomas for lending your name to this work and for lending your voice of counsel down through the years, I am deeply appreciative. To Dr. Lee P. Washington and the Reid Temple AME family, thank you for walking with me as I seek to fulfill the calling on my life. I know prayer works because you all have covered me in prayers and I am grateful.

Introduction

WHY READ THIS BOOK?

Don't tell anyone, but I have had long dry spells when my prayer life was simply dead, on a life support system or in need of rehabilitation. I have discovered that the restoration of my prayer life, as well as my greatest growth spurts in prayer, came as a result of reading books that provided biblical insights into the power and practice of prayer. In other words, knowing *why* I should pray caused me to pray more, and knowing *how* I should pray helped me to pray more effectively. My prayer is that this book will likewise serve as a catalyst in your relationship with God, by igniting your prayer life and helping you to mature in your role as a disciple for Jesus Christ.

WHY 50 DAYS?

Fifty days after Jesus was raised from the dead (Easter), the Holy Spirit fell on the believers who had gathered in Jerusalem (Pentecost). Simon Peter is the central figure on whom Jesus focused before he was crucified, and again after he was resurrected on Easter. Simon Peter also became the pivotal person that led the church after Jesus ascended into heaven and after the Holy Spirit descended upon the believers on the day of Pentecost. Before Jesus was crucified, Simon Peter deserted him. Fifty days later, Simon Peter was Jesus' greatest representative on earth. Peter's transformation happened during those fifty days that Jesus appeared to his followers and gave them further instruction. While his words were challenging to all, they obviously had a special impact on Simon Peter. He now understood why Jesus was crucified, why Jesus had established a succession plan, and that he had a crucial role in that plan. Now remember, Peter had often been privileged to join Jesus during his time of prayer, so it seems obvious that these fifty days must have been an intensive time of prayer for Peter. Just imagine how the Holy Spirit can transform you after spending fifty days in prayer!

WHY LUKE 22:31-32?

This book has been written as a discipleship-strengthening program in the same way that a personal trainer might create a workout program that is designed to achieve specific results. Think of it as a seven-week *"fitness prayer"* program where each day you are given a specific scriptural passage (in the New King James Version translation) as a complement to the Luke 22:31-32 core passage, to use in your devotion time. In this passage, Peter, a disciple of Jesus Christ, is informed that a demonic attack is imminent. What ensues is a faith journey that tests Peter and one where he learns what it means to be prayed for by the Savior, and how that prayer ultimately transforms his life and leads him to greater faith and a concentrated focus on God's Kingdom. Over the course of seven weeks, you will understand the personal value, purpose and power of prayer, and how developing a life of intentional prayer will transform your life. The goals of this book are to advance your spiritual development through inspiration, information and impartation.

Each weekly theme is enhanced daily with additional scriptures and insights to help connect the principle of prayer being shared for the week, to the practice of your prayer. At the end of each devotion is a reflection question to help you draw closer to God as you ignite your prayer life. As you read each section, begin by praying that God will open your heart and mind to be receptive to His word.

TIPS FOR READING

1. **Read the Bible -**This book is based on the word of God, so you will need a Bible to appreciate its full meaning.
2. **Pray -** This book is written both to give inspiration to your prayer life, as well as instruction as to how to pray. Therefore, to benefit from these pages, you must devote your time to both reading and then praying about what you have read.
3. **Don't Do It Alone -**Whether it is in an informal group of friends, through a small group, or as a church-wide initiative, our faith is best when it is shared with others so that iron can sharpen iron. Also, it will hold you accountable to reading and praying every day.

4. **Spread It-** I have included hashtags for each day so that you can engage with others through social media about what the Lord is speaking to you each day.

 **#ignite50Day**

twitter: @matthewwatley

5. **Surf It -** There are additional resources available at www.matthewwatley.com to help bring this 50-day journey alive. Get ready to Ignite!

Luke 22:31-32 (NRSV) "Simon, Simon, listen! Satan has demanded to sift all of you like wheat, (32) but I have prayed for you that your own faith may not fail; and you, when once you have turned back, strengthen your brothers."

Week 1: The Necessity of Confession and Conviction in Prayer
"Simon, Simon, listen!"
Week 2: Prayer is Spiritual Warfare
"Satan has demanded..."
Week 3: Praying for Endurance Through Testing
"to sift all of you like wheat..."
Week 4: The Power of Intercessory Prayer
"but I have prayed for you..."
Week 5: Praying For Faith
"that your own faith may not fail..."
Week 6: The Role of Repentance and Redemption in Prayer
"and you, when you have turned back..."
Week 7: Praying to Fulfill Your Purpose and
Kingdom Assignment
"strengthen your brothers."

Chapter One:
THE NECESSITY OF CONFESSION AND CONVICTION IN PRAYER

"Simon, Simon, listen!"

DAY 1 | LISTEN UP!

MATTHEW 16:13-20
Key Verse: 17

"Jesus answered and said to him, "Blessed are you, Simon Bar-Jonah, for flesh and blood has not revealed this to you, but My Father who is in heaven.""

It is amazing how one word can rewind your life 20 years in the blink of an eye. Before you know it, degrees, jobs, children, awards and the image you have created of yourself as an adult all vanish when you are called by your childhood nickname. You and the caller of your nickname have instantly gone back in time through this bond of familiarity. This can be a good thing or a bad thing depending on what that time in your life was like. Former names may be affectionately labeled or they may be used to intimidate depending who is using them. The names themselves are often telling. Who wouldn't want to hear "it's 'The Boss'," from a familiar voice if you were captain of the football team, or if you were voted most likely to succeed. On the other hand, "hey squirt face" can bring a flood of negative emotions as it takes you back to a time when people called you that to make your life miserable. I guess it all comes down to who is saying your old name, and the reason they are saying it.

In Luke 22:31 the one who is calling Peter by his former name 'Simon' is Jesus. The reason Jesus says Simon! Simon is to call Peter's attention to something of critical significance. Of course, Jesus, more than anyone, would be best qualified to use Peter's former name, because it was in the 16th chapter of Matthew that Jesus actually changed Simon's name to Peter, which means 'rock'. Jesus declared that Peter would be the rock upon which he would build his church. Therefore, for Jesus to refer to Peter by his pre-rock name, not once but twice, is of real importance. Jesus calls him Simon not as an act of demotion, but as a point of access to his original self. God knows and can name our old nature without negating the promise of our new name.

As a child, when my mother called me by my whole name, Matthew Lawrence Watley, I felt instantly on-edge. I knew that whatever she said next was going to be important based on the way she addressed me. Jesus' saying, "Simon, Simon" functioned in the same way.

Prayer is a conversation between you and God and there may be times when God needs to address you in a manner that gets your attention immediately. Just as the long, high-pitched tone and scrolling message on television indicates an alert from the Emergency Broadcast System, we are alerted and pay attention when God refers to our original selves. This is where God may impress upon your heart the identity of someone who needs your prayerful attention, or as with Peter, the Lord may reveal a demonic attack at work in your own life. When God calls you by name, there is only one thing to do. Listen!

Reflection Question

Have you ever felt convicted in prayer...not necessarily about sin, but that God was trying to get your attention? Did you pause in that moment or rush past it?

 #ignite50Day1

DAY 2 | CONFESSION IS GOOD FOR YOUR PRAYER LIFE

GENESIS 2:18-25
Key Verse: 25

And they were both naked, the man and his
wife, and were not ashamed

We all have two selves...our projected self and our actual self. Our projected self is who we claim to be, while our actual self is who we really are authentically. Acknowledging our actual selves, with all of our aspirations, anxieties, sins, and short-comings is really an act of confession. Confession in relation-ship with God means owning who we are, what we have done, and where we are in life. This is the key to a real relationship with God because it serves as a base line for the Holy Spirit to move and operate in our lives. In fact, this was God's original intent for us. Before Adam and Eve succumbed to tempta-tion in the Garden of Eden, the Bible describes them as being *'naked and not ashamed'*. This was a description of not only how they viewed one another, but also how they saw them-selves in the eyes of God. They were each whole. Their ac-tual selves were identical to their projected selves.

Once Adam and Eve chose to disobey God, we see the division of their identities into their actual selves and their pro-jected selves. By covering themselves with leaves, blaming one another and the serpent for their sinful actions, each of them sought to deflect attention from their actual selves and proj-ect a different image than who they really were. Unfortunately, this same deflection of the truth happens in our prayer life. We begin wrong-footed because we seek to relate to God through the mask of our projected selves. We attempt to address God in prayer with impressive or pious-sounding words, not neces-sarily to give reverence to God, but to make ourselves appear more holy than we really are. We are so used to covering and compensating for our weaknesses when interacting with people, that we often take this same approach with God.

God wants to deal with the real us- what I like to call our *Simon-side*, so that God can continue to develop us into who God intends for us to be - our *Peter-side*. One of the roles of the Holy Spirit, who acts as the arbiter of our prayer life, is to allow us a *'Simon, Simon listen'* moment. God cannot speak to our projected self. For real conversation to occur between us and God, He must get to our actual selves. This is the place of conviction that leads to conversation.

Prayer is the only time in life when we can achieve that kind of openness. God is the only one with whom we can risk being *'naked and not ashamed.'* Prayer at its best does not come from the soul of the *in-control, well-put-together self* that we have projected as our adult identity. Prayer comes from the soul of that scared, confused, guilt-ridden child that still lives within each of us. It is when our actual self speaks up in its nakedness and exposes its unhealed wounds and broken places that God is able to truly minister to us by His Spirit.

Reflection Question

Does your prayer life emanate from your actual self, or your projected self?

DAY 3 | CONFESSION IS GOOD FOR YOUR PRAYER LIFE

GENESIS 2:18-25
Key Verse: 13

So David said to Nathan, "I have sinned against the Lord." And Nathan said to David, "The Lord also has put away your sin; you shall not die."

Despite King David's great military, religious, and political leadership, he was still flawed. In one of his most pronounced series of misdeeds, David orchestrates an adulterous affair with Bathsheba, attempts a cover up of her resulting pregnancy, and then has her husband Uriah killed. After this, the prophet Nathan comes to David with a four-word indictment, *"thou art the man"* and calls him out for his sinful deeds. David's response may actually be part of the reason scripture refers to him as *'a man after God's own heart.'* David does not deny his actions or blame someone else; rather he confesses to the crime saying, *"I have sinned against the Lord."*

These are words of transparency and accountability. These are the same words that must regularly proceed from the heart of our prayer life. Every day we disobey God by the unkind words we say, the impure thoughts we think, and the ungodly deeds we do. That's why it is necessary to confess and admit our wrongdoing. Yes, confession goes against our nature. We wrongly think that admitting our misdoings will destroy God's call upon our lives, when in truth it is just the opposite. Our confession causes God to draw more near because now our sin no longer stands between us.

Sometimes it can be hard to admit that we've sinned against someone. Interestingly, although David has acted sinfully against several people, he does not identify them as the object of his sin; rather, David says that his sin is against the Lord. The same is true for us when we sin – it is against God. Though we tend to think the immediate victims of our sinful thoughts, words, and actions may be other people, ultimately it is God who is wounded. Take for instance a child who steals from a classmate. The other classmate has suffered the hurt of the loss of their property, but the little thief's parents have suffered the harm of disappointment and dishonor. Thus, the larger apology is owed to the parent.

As soon as David confessed his sin, Nathan responded immediately by telling David, *"the Lord has put away your sin."* Nathan's statement about God's forgiveness of David is difficult to accept given the severity of David's confession. Our fundamental sense of fairness asks how an adulterer, a deceiver, and a murderer can be so quickly forgiven. The answer is difficult for us to conceive because it is based on a spiritual truth. When we disappoint and dishonor our Heavenly Father, He has every right to disown us, but His love for us will not allow Him to do so. Instead, He is eager to forgive us so that our relationship with Him might be fully restored.

When a child sincerely apologizes, a loving parent usually forgives instantly, even though there still may be ramifications resulting from the wrong that has been done. Confession cures the crisis of conviction but not necessarily the consequences. When we confess our sins in prayer, God is quick to forgive us because He knows that we will need Him even more as we face the consequences of our actions.

Reflection Question

What is it that you need to confess so that God can forgive it?

DAY 4 | DON'T PUFF UP! COME AS YOU ARE TO GOD

LUKE 18:9-14
Key Verse: 13

And the tax collector, standing afar off, would not so much as raise his eyes to heaven, but beat his breast, saying, "God, be merciful to me a sinner!"

Puffer fish are one of God's most interesting creations. These fish, when fearful, fill themselves with large amounts of water, increasing their body by several sizes, and presenting spike-like protrusions. This God-given ability causes the fish to appear like a troubling target for any would-be predator. Of course with all things in life, there is a downside to this ability. The puffer all but loses its mobility. Filled with water, and losing its streamlined shape, it is not able to quickly swim and turn as it would normally. Likewise, we too, often choose to puff ourselves up out of fear, attempting to make ourselves appear larger than we really are. We don't realize that when we are all puffed up, we are unable to make any forward progress. No place is this more evident than in our relationship with God. The puffed up, haughty, prideful presence that we have created for ourselves, or the self we try to mask with false humility, is really a sign of insecurity-an overcompensation tactic for a fear which we seek to hide.

In Luke 18, Jesus shares a parable of a puffed up person. This Pharisee, who prayed boasting of his personal exploits, seemed convinced that the things that look impressive in the eyes of people would somehow impress God. Not only did he see himself as great, but also saw himself as being greater than others. One such person was a tax collector who had come to pray at the same time. He stood far off, beat his breast and confessed his sinful state. Jesus points out that only the tax collector's prayer would be regarded because it came from his actual self.

The joy of prayer is that it is our most unguarded time of the day and it is an exercise in humility. The prototypical posture of prayer, bowing and bending on one's knees with hands clasped together, is a visible symbol of someone begging. Beggars are without pride or pretense. They are desperate and shout their need for help. This is the one who gets God's attention, for the bible says that God resists the proud, but gives grace to the humble. The proud, by their posture, oppose the assistance of God. The humble welcome God's attention, and by their admission of lack, God readily responds with grace.

Reflection Question

What prideful part of your personality is preventing God's presence in your life?

DAY 5 | WHO IS CALLING YOUR NAME?

1 SAMUEL 3: 8-10
Key Verse: 10

Now the Lord came and stood and called as at other times, "Samuel! Samuel!" And Samuel answered, "Speak, for Your servant hears."

A friend of mine had sons who insisted on getting a dog. Even though he was not particularly fond of the creatures, he yielded and got the boys a dog. They named the dog Brownie and enjoyed rough-housing, walking, and taking care of him. My friend and Brownie had a cordial but not particularly warm relationship. One day Brownie escaped from the yard, and with the youngest son chasing, soon disappeared from their neighborhood. The boys alerted their father, who grudgingly got in the car and began scouring the surrounding neighborhoods, with the boys calling out for their beloved pet.

After some time had passed, they found Brownie, who rather than running toward them, ran away. Now they were in hot pursuit, with the father driving, the boys yelling, and Brownie racing. Soon, Brownie found himself cornered between houses and fences. The older son jumped out to grab Brownie, but stopped in his tracks when Brownie growled and barked. The boy froze, but in an instant the father was out of the car, and in a loud stern voice said, "Brownie get in this car!" Brownie immediately dropped his tail and ears and jumped into the back seat of the car. Once in the car, he returned to his playful and loving self. The boys were confused, and asked their dad why Brownie acted this way. After all they were friends - they played with him, and took care of him. Their father explained that when Brownie ran away he became scared and confused. He went on to say that the dog was not looking for a friend at that time, but rather was looking for someone in authority – a leader who could help him. When he heard the dad's voice he knew it was the voice of someone in charge.

Isn't there great joy in knowing that Jesus does not call us servant, but calls us friend. Even so, we must remember that there are times when Jesus cannot stand in the role of friend because there are times when we desperately need him as a leader - times when we need someone in authority over us that we can look to, and who we feel compelled to obey. When Jesus says *'Listen!'* to Simon Peter, he is not making a request; rather, he is giving a command. Commands are only significant when they come from one of authority to another who falls under that authority.

Reflection Question

How do you respond when you hear God's voice calling out to you?

DAY 6 | TELL GOD YOUR REAL FEELINGS ABOUT YOUR SITUATION

LUKE 22:39-46
Key Verse: 42

"Father, if it is Your will, take this cup away from Me; nevertheless not My will, but Yours be done."

I am part of an accountability group that helps me to stay focused on my faith. It is comprised of a small number of male pastors. The group is not as "formal" as you might expect. We do not have regular meeting times, but we talk regularly. We don't do Bible studies together, but we always discuss scripture. And, we're more likely to get together to shoot trap or billiards and engage in idle conversation rather than some deep introspective dialogue. Even so, each of us knows that in times of difficulty we can call on the group and share our concerns, and when issues of disquiet arise we take it upon ourselves to follow up with the member in crisis. We pray together on matters of ministry and family, and genuinely enjoy one another's company as friends.   Early in the formation of this group, we came up with a phrase that typifies our unique dynamic. One brother was sharing with us about a relationship he was considering. While he was rationalizing and justifying the obvious red flags this relationship raised, finally, after a lengthy dialogue, one of us said, "Listen, lie to us but tell yourself the truth." The point was simple. It was obvious that he was being disingenuous with us, but the larger concern was that he was being disingenuous with himself.

When we look at Jesus' experience in the Garden of Gethsemane, we see a powerful example of transparency before God and honesty with oneself. His prayer lays bare before God the true issue that he is wrestling with at this point in his life - namely his death on the Cross. He does not want to be crucified. Jesus seeks an act of clemency from God the Father. Yet, he is honestly torn because he also wants to redeem humanity from sin once and for all. His question is "can this be accomplished by any other method?"

It does not sound very noble. It seems as if he is looking for a way around the self-sacrifice and he is. Like Jesus, in our own lives it is not sinful to acknowledge the difficulty or even lack of desire to complete our assignments in God. The point of our prayer life is to work through these difficult moments with the Lord and pray to receive both instruction and empowerment in order to do God's will. When we are honest with God, God can strengthen us, even surrounding us with angels to complete the task for which we have been created and called.

One of the joys of a healthy prayer life is that it allows us to find our voice. One of the great joys of my life is hanging out with my daughter. She is at the age where she is able to verbally express what she's feeling without being burdened by trying to make her thoughts palatable, non-offensive, or politically correct. She thinks it and she says it. As her father, I am not offended by what she says because there is nothing she can ever say to alter my love for her. I also recognize that she is only saying what she feels as opposed to masking it the way the rest of us have learned to do.

Having a healthy prayer life is like that – having the freedom to express to God what you are feeling. I believe the reason Jesus could speak so boldly to the Father was because he understood that God's love was unwavering and to do anything less would be disingenuous. I challenge you to become unvarnished and unfiltered in your prayer life. Your real feelings of anger, fear and frustration are all great things to share with God. He knows how you feel anyway, but when you express it, you grant Him permission to draw near and help you through it.

Reflection Question

What is it that God knows about you, that you've never expressed to him?

DAY 7 | RECOGNIZING GOD'S VOICE

JOHN 10:22-29
Key Verse: 27
"My sheep hear my voice. I know them,
and they follow me."

If you are blessed enough to have parents whom you communicate with regularly, I would suspect that when you talk on the phone they do not begin by saying, "Hi, this is your father or mother." There is no need for them to identify themselves because of the nature of your relationship. Each of you is familiar with the other's voice.

That's what Jesus wants from us – for us to recognize his voice when he calls us. Jesus uses the phrase, '*Simon, Simon, listen!*' to establish the familiarity of his voice so that Peter's ear might be attuned to hearing what the Lord has to say. Just as it is important to confess our sins, it is also important to hear from our Heavenly Father.

Prayer is not just about talking. It is also about listening. Hearing from God about the decisions we must make, or revealing the hurts or fears of the *actual selves* of persons in our lives, requires hearing, knowing, and listening to God's voice. Should I allow my loved one to languish in a vegetative state, or should I authorize the doctor to pull the plug? Should I continue to work through this marriage, or is enough *enough*? What do I do with my child who is spiraling out of control? How do I reconcile my sexual desires with the witness of scripture? None of these questions has a patent answer. Each must be worked through in a constant dialogue with God. The key is to honestly distinguish between God's divine voice, and the voice of our deeply held desires or fear. It is only through regular relational communication that we are able to distinguish the true voice of God from the many other voices in our lives and within our own souls.

One of the scariest moments of parenthood is when you find yourself channeling your own parents. You open your mouth, but it's your parents' words that come out. That's because those words have become engrained in your spirit and are now foundational to who you are. One of the ways we know God's voice is by recognizing what He has already said in scripture. Often times, people struggle to hear God's voice because they do not have His word engrained in their hearts. We know God will not contradict Himself; therefore, voices that speak contrary to the word of God are obviously not of God.

Sheep follow the familiar voice of their shepherd. They do not pick up their heads to see where they are going. They simply follow the shepherd's leading based on what he says and on his proximity to them. They have learned that following his voice leads to provision and protection. Likewise, the shepherd knows his sheep, and keeps his eye on key members of the flock. The constant stragglers, the leaders and the wanderers all warrant special attention and often are the object of specific commands. The joy of an abundant prayer life is that God speaks to us, His sheep, in specific ways to provide us direction.

Reflection Question

How do you recognize God's voice in your life? What assures you that it's His voice and not your own?

Chapter Two:

PRAYER IS SPIRITUAL WARFARE

"Satan has demanded..."

DAY 8 | LET YOUR PRAYER FIGHT YOUR BATTLE

LUKE 22:31-32
Key Verse: 32
But I have prayed for you that
your own faith may not fail.

Jesus' words here are some of the most disturbing in scripture. To begin with, Jesus identifies the devil by name as a real figure who desires to work evil in Simon Peter's life just as he does in ours. God's word provides Satan's resume, declaring that he comes "but to kill, to steal, and to destroy." The truth is, just like Peter, we will all find ourselves under satanic attack. If this were not sufficiently disturbing, Jesus' next words will send chills down your spine. He says, "Satan has demanded to sift you like wheat..." The imagery here is of Satan coming to God strongly petitioning God to allow him access to Peter. Another translation of this same phrase is more disturbing. It may be interpreted that Satan has obtained permission to sift you like wheat. It's one thing to know what Satan desires to do, yet it's another to be told that he's been granted permission to do it.

Fortunately, as disturbing as these words are, we also find hope in them when we consider their implications. First, by identifying Satan by name, it is clear that Jesus is acutely aware of the identity and even the plans of our adversary. We take great comfort when the doctor names the disorder from which we are suffering. It tells us that we are on a known path and not dealing with an unknown quantity. Second, the fact that "Satan has demanded..." shows the limitation of his power. The best tactics of war do not happen with someone asking for permission to attack. To do so, it is at the sole discretion of the aggressor, and is generally based on his ability to inflict damage upon the enemy.

While certainly Satan is our adversary, he cannot unilaterally act in or lives without first petitioning God. This of course begs the question presented by the interpretation "has received permission," why would God grant the devil permission to sift Peter, or you and me? Allowing is very different than approving. There are many things parents *allow* that they do not *approve* of which may actually be hurtful to their children. That's because parents understand it is only through some suffering, some struggling, and difficulty that their children will learn the necessary lessons for proper living. Of course there is a limit. No parent will allow their child to be destroyed simply to teach a lesson. Therefore, the scope of whatever the parent allows is always limited.

These disturbing words are a call for the believer to take action through prayer. Prayer in times of satanic attack bolsters the spirit of those who find solace in knowing they are not fighting by themselves. Prayer does more than simply calm our fears -it changes the nature of the fight. Battle plans never survive the initial engagement with the enemy. Once the adversary is identified, prayer works to alter his plans or the results of his plans.

Reflection Question

What battles are you facing today or what attacks are coming against you?

DAY 9 | SPARRING AGAINST THE ENEMY

EPHESIANS 6:10-20
Key Verse: 12

For we do not wrestle against flesh and blood, but against principalities, against powers, against the rulers of the darkness of this age, against spiritual hosts of wickedness in the heavenly places.

Winston Churchill's key contribution to World War II was not politically or even militarily based. Churchill understood the fundamental nature of the German war machine which was driven by an obsessive, fundamentally destructive, evil mad man named Adolph Hitler. While many within England, and other countries as well, sought to figure out what reasonable concession could be made with the German leader that would stave off a global conflict, Churchill knew Hitler would settle for nothing less than world capitulation. As a consequence, he resolved that the utter defeat of Germany would be the only way to achieve the security of the world.

Whenever we fail to understand the fundamental nature of conflict, we limit ourselves in its resolution. In Ephesians, Paul acknowledges the fundamental nature of conflict as being spiritual. Whether one is dealing with conflict with co-workers or between nations, we must recognize that beneath it all is a spiritual contest. Therefore, prayer must be engaged as a spiritual weapon. Prayer fortifies our faith in God's ultimate authority over every issue so we do not overly concern ourselves with human authority. Prayer provides us the opportunity to receive intelligence as to the actual motivations and agendas of those whose actions would otherwise remain inscrutable. Prayer bolsters our strength through the inevitable battles that will be lost on the path to our ultimate victory.

Evil, whether cloaked or obvious, is ruthless in its intent. Evil does not seek to establish an amicable agreement. Therefore, half-measures and concessions will never stave off demonic attacks. Passivity on our part makes the aggressor more aggressive. Still, we must be careful not to become so focused on evil that it distracts us from our real purpose -our real victory. Defeat of evil is not victory. Victory is when we fulfill our God-given purpose, part of which will require us to triumph over demonic attacks. Paul's point is for us to neither focus on the individuals that may do evil toward us, nor even the places from which evil arises. Like Churchill, we must be prepared to fight on every front.

Reflection Question

What things are you struggling against – and are you ready to use prayer to help you fight it?

DAY 10 | ARE YOU UP FOR THE TEST?

JOB 1:6-12
Key Verse: 8

The LORD said to Satan "Have you considered my servant Job? There is no one like him on the earth, a blameless and upright man who fears God and turns away from evil."

In this passage, God nominates Job to Satan for testing based on Job's character. This passage seems counter-intuitive because we generally think of God as the one who gets us *out* of trouble, not the one who gets us *into* trouble. It says a lot about how far we have strayed from the biblical notion of suffering. For a faith that makes the Cross its primary symbol to have so distanced itself from innocent suffering is amazing. Of course to be fair to the text, it should be pointed out that clearly Satan was already seeking to test someone.

God's nomination of Job is to prove Job's faithfulness rather than arbitrarily cause him to suffer. Even in our suffering, God has the ability to set limits on our duress. The larger point is that demonic attacks come with being a child of God. Let that sink in! If your expectation is that being saved will make life easier, there are hosts of biblical figures and numerous Christians throughout the centuries that will correct you of this notion.

I remember growing up, like many of my generation, being enamored by certain products advertised on television which seemed like a great value given the quality of the product and the low purchase price. What I did not realize then was often in life things are not as wonderful as they appear. Many times, the price that is quoted is not the only cost to the consumer. One might find there are exorbitant shipping and handling fees, other hidden costs, or the customer has become locked into an extended contract requiring him to purchase other products that he did not want. The fine print of these deals often creates a much different situation than the one that first appeared so wonderful.

Sometimes I fear we seek to *sell* Christianity through similar means. We advertise the new and abundant life that is found in Christ, the joy of the Holy Spirit living in us, the Kingdom access, and the authority we have as heirs of the Father. Yet, there is more to this *deal* than the many spiritual and practical benefits. There is what I like to refer to as the "fine print of the faith." The fine print has to do with things like suffering for the gospel and having to sacrifice aspects of our lifestyle that are not consistent with our new lives in Christ.

Of course knowing suffering is part of the inheritance of the believer does not make it more palatable, but it does make it bearable. Jesus made clear the fine print of the faith in Matthew 5:11-12, *"Blessed are you when people revile you and persecute you and utter all kinds of evil against you falsely on my account. ¹² Rejoice and be glad, for your reward is great in heaven, for in the same way they persecuted the prophets who were before you."*

Jesus' words make it clear that evil is real and will attack us because of who we are in God. One of the roles of prayer is to lay bare our feelings of frustration as we unfairly suffer from lies and attacks when we have done nothing wrong. In prayer our faith finds the blessedness that Jesus promises as a part of the process. After we move past the emotional response to being wrongly reviled and persecuted, we find ourselves forced into a greater position of dependence on God for our protection and even our exoneration. Amazingly, whether we are ultimately delivered is not the primary point. The blessedness comes through the greater dependence. This is a mystery of faith that can only be attained through the word of God, faith in God, and a strong prayer life.

Reflection Question

Are you willing to suffer as a Christian, knowing that the promises of Jesus will protect you?

DAY 11 | NEVER GIVE UP!

GALATIANS 6:7-10
Key Verse: 9
And let us not grow weary while doing
good, for in due season we shall reap
if we do not lose heart.

World War I is considered a classic example of a "war of attrition." The armies literally fought from entrenched positions which caused battles to drag on for months as neither side was able to gain a quick, decisive advantage that would put their enemy on its' heels. In this kind of combat, the victor is the one who has greater supplies of armaments, foodstuff, and manpower. Tactics and maneuvers take a backseat to the supply chain and the will to hold on through the mounting carnage. Spiritual warfare often takes on the characteristics of a war of attrition.

Winning in spiritual warfare comes down to this one phrase, *"if you don't quit, you will win."* Spiritual warfare is generally long and drawn out because most of us are very formidable in our faith over short periods of time. However, when hours become weeks, and those weeks turn into years, we have a tendency to surrender our hope, our expectations, and even our faith. We choose to self-protect by lowering our expectations to match our reality. Rather than being drained by holding on to the disappointments of our current lives with one hand, and our future hopes with the other, it is easier to believe that the way things are is the way they will always be.

The devil acts in specific ways in his attempt to defeat our faith. He will use deception, temptation, or even accusation; however, one of his favorite tactics is delay. He seeks to exploit our lack of patience and endurance. Paul's admonishment to "*be not weary in well doing,*" ends with a promise of harvest, "*for you shall reap if you faint not.*" The principle of sowing and reaping is found throughout scripture, and is employed here to recast our understanding of the significance of being consistent in the well-doing of sowing spiritual seed.

Whenever a seed is planted it must germinate and grow before there can be any fruit, grain, or flower to be harvested. We must simply hold on in faith until the harvest is ready. Prayer is the key to this holding on. Talking with God persuades us of His reality and surety. Lack of contact in any relationship fosters fear and doubt, and undermines trust and love. When we are waiting for God to move, it is important to talk to God in the interim. Prayer provides the nutrients and life-giving water to the seed of faith. Prayer rushes resources and reinforcements to the frontline of the battle.

Reflection Question

What long-term battle are you facing for which you need to enlist the power of prayer?

#ignite50Day11

35

DAY 12 | THE LORD HAS PRAYED FOR YOU

LUKE 22:31-32
Key Verse: 32
But I have prayed for you, that your faith
should not fail;

As a believer, you must never forget that not only has God given you a specific purpose to fulfill, but he has also allowed specific problems to teach you to survive. Just as each of us has a unique Kingdom assignment, we also are burdened with a unique Kingdom attack. In each case, we can be confident because we understand that we have been specifically equipped in our unique design of who we are to meet each challenge. Where some would become unnerved by certain challenges, others are encouraged. Our faith is strangely braced by the new onslaught of negative circumstances. The curious explanation is clear – we were made for this moment. Jesus' prayer for Peter's faith distinguishes his anticipated response to this crisis of faith from the other believers. Our Lord's focus is that while other's faith will fail, Peter's will succeed.

Nature provides us with myriad examples of how the particularity of design allows not simply survival, but the ability to thrive in places where other life forms cannot survive. Cacti, polar bears, mountain goats, and blue whales each have the same testimony - that there are things about their makeup that allow them to flourish where other creatures cannot endure. It is easy to lapse into a self-pitying-victimization mindset when we find ourselves facing extreme difficulties. Lingering sicknesses, hostile work environments, and dysfunctional relationships can all seem so daunting that losing hope is not only easy, it is logical. However, this is when we must be confident in the uniqueness of our faith make up. We must be assured that if God has allowed certain circumstance in our lives, it is because He is certain that we can endure them.

This is where our prayer life takes holds. When we fail to have confidence in ourselves to be equal to the challenges before us, we must pray for confidence in God's choice to allow it. Sometime ago while working out, I was challenged by my trainer to complete an exercise that I knew was beyond my capacity. Rather than trusting my perception of my strength, I trusted my trainer's opinion of my capacity. And what do you know - I completed the task rather easily. In times of trouble, through prayer, we can hear God say, "*you were made for this fight, and you're going to win!*"

Reflection Question

What situation is God saying to you "*you were made for this fight and you're going to win?*"

DAY 13 | "Get Behind Me, Satan"

Matthew 16:13-23
Key Verse: 23

But He turned and said to Peter, "Get behind Me, Satan! You are an offense to Me, for you are not mindful of the things of God, but the things of men."

Not long after Jesus proclaimed Simon to be Peter, the rock of the church, did he then begin to talk about the fact that he was going to be crucified and hanged on a Cross. Simon Peter then spoke up and said, let this never happen. Jesus rebuked him, referring to him not as Simon or as Peter, but saying, "*get behind me Satan, you are an offense to Me, for you are not mindful of the things of God, but the things of men.*"

Despite the fact that Simon Peter had left his family and business to follow Jesus, had received the revelation of Jesus as Messiah, and received a new name, he was never the less co-opted by Satan. This is a reminder to us that neither our salvation nor our spiritual gifts will keep us from being affected and influenced by the devil.

One of my favorite sermon illustrations is to stand on the stage in church while someone stands on the stairs, maybe a step or two below where I stand while we hold hands. Then I pose the question to the congregation, "will it be easier for me to pull the other person up or for them to pull me down." Of course the laws of physics give the strong advantage to the one who is standing on the stairs. My point is simply that oftentimes, it is those to whom we are connected that ultimately have the advantage to hold us down from spiritual ascent. Satan's strategy was to use Peter to encourage Jesus from sacrificing himself on the Cross. One writer says that "the devil uses people to introduce spirits into vessels that he wants to control."

We will see later in the Gospel writings that Jesus had his own feelings of trepidation about his crucifixion and that Peter was being used by Satan to fan the flames of those fears. As believers we must be mindful that prayer extinguishes the flames of fear that are stoked by individuals who are close to us, but who may unwittingly be co-opted by evil influence. Don't picture a friend who practices Satanism. Think of it as someone who is a Christian and loves you dearly, yet who may feel that your sacrifices for ministry in time, talent, or treasure are simply too much. In this kind of situation, your prayer will help to quickly discard these attempts to derail God's purpose for your life, and prayer will then bolster your courage so that you re-double your commitment to living a life of faith.

The older saints in the church where I grew up used to call this kind of consistency and fervency of prayer life as being *"prayed up."* When I am "prayed up" I am less likely to be influenced by individuals who are not divinely-minded, but human-minded. When I'm prayed up, I feel empowered to speak the truth in love about things and people that are contrary to God's word and will. When I'm "prayed up" I am able to distinguish between what is personal and what is spiritual.

Reflection Question

How has your faith impacted your most important and intimate relationships?

DAY 14 | YOU'RE IN A FIXED FIGHT

REVELATION 12: 7-12
Key Verse: 7

And war broke out in heaven: Michael and his angels fought with the dragon; and the dragon and his angels fought

There was a beautiful tree that grew in the yard of an ordinary house. It was so striking that a man used to drive by this house just to see the tree. The owner obviously appreciated the tree's beauty because he went through great lengths to protect it. He built a high fence with a locked gate, and placed a barking dog on the inside. One day, the man's drive came to an unexpected stop as he looked to see the beloved tree only to discover that the gate was open, the dog put away, and there were men tearing down the tree.

Although they had never met, the driver pulled over to inquire of the owner as to why he would allow this tree to be destroyed. The owner could tell that the driver was sincere so he walked him over to one of the branches that had already been taken down, and pulled back the bark to reveal that termites had eaten out the core of the tree. Unseen termites had gone under the high fence, past the locked gate, and paid no attention to the barking dog. Though it still appeared beautiful on the outside, there was drama in the darkness.

There is nothing that we can do to protect or insulate ourselves from destruction and demonic attack. No matter what we have, who we are, or even where we are, evil breaks every barrier in order to cause chaos in our lives. Revelation 12 informs us that of all places for it to happen, war broke out in heaven with Satan represented as the dragon, contending against Michael the archangel. If the devil caused problems in heaven, then it stands to reason that there's no place on earth safe from his influence. Thus our prayer lives should not simply focus on trying to arrive at a new, *'safer'* place in life, but rather wherever we are, we must pray that we can withstand the inevitable demonic attacks. There is no community we can move to, no church we can join, and no circle of family and friends that evil influences will not penetrate. While we certainly should aspire to places and people of spiritual safety, we do so recognizing that there is no perfectly secure place.

We should not become fearful or paranoid. Even though Revelation 12 informs us of the spiritual battle that broke out in heaven, it also tells us that the dragon was defeated. Being a believer does not mean that we will not have to fight. It just means that in the end, God grants us victory over the devil. In fact, God sends angelic assistance to aid our cause in times of attack. This means that victory is not based on our strength of endurance, wisdom or courage. When we find ourselves in difficult seasons the Holy Spirit whispers to us in prayer that *"the battle is not yours, it's the Lord's."*

Reflection Question

Are you able to trust God to fight your battles or are you more likely to take matters into your own hands?

Chapter Three:
PRAYING FOR ENDURANCE THROUGH TESTING

"to sift all of you all like wheat"

DAY 15 | ...IT'S NOT ABOUT YOU – IT'S ABOUT GOD'S PURPOSE FOR YOU

LUKE 22:31-32
Key Verse: 31-32

And the Lord said, "Simon, Simon! Indeed, Satan has asked for you, that he may sift you as wheat. But I have prayed for you, that your faith should not fail; and when you have returned to Me, strengthen your brethren."

Satan's petition to God is to sift Simon Peter. Of course sifting is the process of shaking that causes separation. Satan's plan is to shake Simon Peter as an individual so that he becomes separated from God and from his Godly purpose. But in the original Greek, the word *you* is plural, which means that Satan's goal is to separate God from God's church. Notice that Satan's plan and his goal are connected and distinct. His focus is on Peter because of Peter's pivotal role in God's plan as being the rock of the church. Ultimately if Simon Peter falls, the net result of Satan's plan against Peter will allow him to reach his ultimate goal which is to sift or separate God's church from him.

Jesus is warning and informing Simon Peter that he is the subject of Satan's plan, but the church is the object. Satan's attack affects you but it is not about you. There is always a larger goal - which is God's purpose in you. Think of it this way. Safes and vaults are not destroyed because people hate them. They are manipulated, blown apart, and assaulted because people desire to possess what they contain. Peter's purpose in God, as the rock of the church, put him in the direct cross hairs of Satan so that with his fall, Satan might abort the church before she could be birthed. It is not enough for us to recognize the attack – we must always remember the point of the attack so that we are sure to protect what is most valuable rather than respond to things that are not central or essential to our survival. The purpose of sin is to draw us away from the presence, power, and purposes of God. Sin is the ultimate distraction (Satan's plan) that leads to destruction (Satan's goal).

The Bible gives us confirmation that the warning that Jesus gave about Satan demanding permission to sift or separate had been granted. In John 21 we see Simon Peter being separated as he announces to his fellow disciples "*I am going fishing.*" And as a testament to Peter's influential leadership, the other disciples go with him. Now this is a curious thing. Even when heading in the wrong direction, Peter's gift and calling as a leader is without repentance. Since they were not all fishermen this trip was not vocational. They were not in a position to afford luxuries, so this was not recreational. It was spiritual. They were literally leaving the way, the Kingdom, and the word as they followed Simon Peter whose faith had obviously been extremely shaken by Jesus' crucifixion. The sifting that started with him was now leading to their collective separation from the faith.

Whenever we are sifted and shifted we must be aware of how we are affected, but remain focused on our purpose. Jesus' words to Simon Peter are not simply to inform him of the pending attack, but to reinforce his assignment. This is where an active prayer life is worth its weight in gold. Prayer helps to span the gap between my feeling and my calling. When being shaken, I feel fatigued and ready to give in. Confessing these feelings makes them available for God to address. While at the same time my prayer life reinforces my resolve to remain true to my calling whether it is a ministry in the church, changing the tide of negative outcomes in my family, or witnessing to Christ's changing power on my job.

Reflection Question

How do you hold steadfast to God in times when you feel you are being sifted by the enemy?

#ignite50Day15

DAY 16 | PROVING GOD

JOB 1:1-12 & MARK 1:9-13

Key Verses:

Job 1:8 Then the Lord said to Satan, "Have you considered My servant Job, that there is none like him on the earth, a blameless and upright man, one who fears God and shuns evil?"

Mark 1:11 Then a voice came from heaven, "You are My beloved Son, in whom I am well pleased."

In the first chapters of Job and Mark, Satan is presented as having negotiated limited access to test an individual. The word for test is the same as trial, which is the same as proof. The last iteration is important because a proof is a confirmation of a prediction. God predicts the character of Job saying he is a just and upright man. God predicts the character of Jesus saying this is my beloved son in whom I am well pleased. And Jesus has already predicted the character of Peter, saying you are '*Petros*' and upon this rock I will build my church. Thus, it is important to remember that what is a test for the believer is the sifting or testing conducted by Satan which results in proving the prediction of God.

It has been my experience that most of the prayers we offer to God fall squarely in the area of testing or trial. The context of the prayer may be because of illness or relationship strife, or financial hardship or religious persecution. God's word reminds us that this time of testing is to *demonstrate* the response of the faith as individuals to the trouble that we are experiencing. Whenever God allows access to the adversary for sifting or testing, it is an expression of God's confidence in the character of faith in that individual. In fact, the time-testing trial and subsequent proving is to demonstrate God's deposit to the believer – the deposit of faith that God has made within him or her.

When we are enduring hard trials and testing, our prayer life becomes our lifeline to God. Its regular practice replenishes our confidence in Him by activating the faith that He has placed on the inside of us. Through their lives of difficult tests and trials, both Jesus and Job regularly prayed to God. Often their prayers were very matter-of-fact, and expressed their personal frustrations, questions, and complaints. Yet, ultimately they were spiritually victorious and God's predictions about them were proven.

Reflection Question

How is your prayer life impacting your faith especially when the enemy is testing you?

DAY 17 | MY GOD, MY GOD!

PSALM 22:1-31 & MATTHEW 27:44-46

Key Verses:

Psalm 22: 1 "My, God, My God, why have You forsaken Me? Why are You So far from helping Me, And from the words of My groaning?"

Matthew 27:44 And about the ninth hour Jesus cried out with a loud voice, saying, "Eli, Eli, lama sabachthani?" that is, "My God, My God, why have You forsaken Me?"

One of the reasons the Psalms are so popular is not simply because of their poetic form, but because the psalmist often is transparent about how it feels to be sifted and to go through various trials. One of the oft overlooked blessings of prayer is its cathartic capacity. In prayer we are free to complain, whine, and express every ounce of frustration and anxiety to a compassionate, big-hearted and loving God. We do not need to mask or sugarcoat our feelings even when we feel betrayed by people or by God. In the final analysis, God already knows how we feel. The only question is whether we will acknowledge those feelings so that they do not possess us, or will we cover them up with nice-sounding words, sentencing ourselves to having to continue to carry them.

The greatest example of the transparency of the psalmist is in Psalm 22:1 where the writer accuses God of forsaking him. No greater charge can be laid against God's character than this. And to make matters worse, the psalmist is not the only one in scripture to level such a charge. Jesus quotes the first line of this very same psalm while he hangs on the Cross. There are several important lessons that we must note. First, we must note that feeling God-forsaken is part of the inheritance of every believer, even to the point where Jesus himself could not die without experiencing this gut-wrenching feeling.

Second, that such statements do not negate or nullify our faith relationship with God, but are evidence of our faith relationship, in that the charge *"forsaker"* is addressed to "My God, My God." Third, while the psalmist and Jesus both made these statements, these were not their final words. The psalmist continues to waver back and forth in Psalm 22 between complaining against God to having confidence in God. Likewise, Jesus would go on to speak three more words from the cross ultimately committing his spirit into the hands of God.

Real prayer is the wrestling that takes place with our own faith in God, particularly when we feel forsaken. At any given moment a sound bite of our prayer may find us leveling charges against God as being a "forsaker," unloving, or unkind. These instances are not the sum total of our prayer life, and God is more than able to address each of these complaints. The key is to continue the conversation with God until He moves us beyond that place. On television we often see a person depicted who is upset and yelling into a phone, and then quickly hanging up after she has finished her rant, offering no opportunity for the other person to respond. If we complain against God, we should not hang up; instead we should stay on our knees for God to respond. The psalmist does exactly this in Psalm 22, going back and forth in his faith, until ultimately he concludes this chapter. Of course in chapter 23 he is well beyond calling God a forsaker, as he begins by writing his most famous and beloved line, "the Lord is my shepherd, I shall not want."

Reflection Question

In what areas of your life do you need to be transparent before God, expressing all of your emotions?

DAY 18 | PRAY FOR THE SHEPHERD OF THE CHURCH

ZECHARIAH 13:7 & MATTHEW 26:31-35

Key Verses:

Zechariah 13:7 "Awake, O sword, against My Shepherd, Against the Man who is My Companion," Says the Lord of hosts. "Strike the Shepherd, And the sheep will be scattered; Then I will turn My hand against the little ones."
Matthew 26:31 "I will strike the Shepherd, And the sheep of the flock will be scattered"

The shaking of the church begins with the shaking of its leadership. At this point Peter has been named as the rock of the church, so any attempt at sifting the church should rightly be directed at Peter. Jesus said as much when he quoted Zechariah, *"strike the shepherd and the sheep will scatter."* The strategy behind striking the shepherd is based on the understanding that the sheep are dependent on the shepherd for their survival. Therefore it is incumbent upon believers to pray for our leaders. Whenever spiritual leaders fail in their faith or fall into sin, persons may fall away from the faith or never even come to the faith. One of the realities today is that it is much easier for Christian ministers to be infamous than to be famous. Therefore, we are obliged to pray for our spiritual leaders who can never be perfect, but still can be used by God to do great things.

The other day I went to see my physician. While he was examining me, he seemed to present several symptoms that indicated that he was not in the best of health. His eyes were glassy, he kept clearing his throat, and he seemed to perspire ever so slightly. My assessment of him turned out to be accurate as he shared with me that he was feeling under the weather. At this point, even though he is the one who provides my primary care, I did not gather up my belongings and storm out of his office just because he was sick. Instead I whispered a prayer for him, fully answered all of his questions and submitted to his exam, and gladly followed his instructions after leaving his office. My point is that a sick doctor can help me get well. In fact he may be of more help since he can readily relate to my own condition. Likewise, God can use imperfect people to accomplish his perfect will. Understand that this is not an endorsement or a license for leaders to sin, but it is a calling for each of us to pray for those who are charged with supporting our spiritual health.

The key is for spiritual leaders not to be more confident than they should be in the strength of their own faith, and for us as believers to offer loving grace to others even as we have received. Of course there are times when failures in ministry require removal and other actions of accountability, but in these instances we are called to pray for these shepherds all the more.

Reflection Question

What specific prayer for your church leaders will you include in your daily devotional times?

DAY 19 | Praying Your Way Through the Trials

Key Verses: JAMES 1:2-4

"My brothers and sisters, whenever you face trials of any kind, consider it nothing but joy, [3]because you know that the testing of your faith produces endurance; [4]and let endurance have its full effect, so that you may be mature and complete, lacking in nothing."

The injury of a super star athlete in sports has literally become an international news event. First the initial injury is replayed repeatedly, and then the announcers feign concern for about thirty seconds before they begin to speculate about how long it will take for the person to recover. For the next few months or maybe even a year, all privacy is lost on the player's part, with doctors who have never examined the person offering television prognoses. Once the surgery is performed, rehabilitation has been completed, medical and legal sign-offs have occurred, the athlete is added back to the roster. They get back on the floor, or field, or ice. Yet they don't play the whole game. They're put in for a few minutes. Afterward, they are asked why they didn't play longer, and the response is always the same. *I'm trying to build up my endurance, trying to get back up to speed.*

What they are saying is that there is nothing that can replace the experience of the real game, and the mind and body have to adjust, by building up cardiovascular capacity to play at their optimal level. There is a hard and fast rule in sports that says technique can be taught, but endurance must be earned.

Spiritually, nothing can take the place of the real challenges of life and faith. Personal tragedies and spiritual crises tax our souls and our faith to the extent that theoretical belief cannot replicate. James 1 seems to take this very utilitarian approach, that is, an approach that the actions are right if they are useful, to understanding trouble and trial. James views suffering as a reason for celebration (count it all joy). Obviously, James is not suggesting that the event itself, death, abuse, betrayal, or disappointment are laudable, nor are the feelings they illicit (pain, disillusionment, fear, hopelessness) meant to be joyous. James is not commending the initial problem or the resulting pain, or even the process of surviving the difficulty. James is commending the product of that suffering - endurance. This endurance is mature and complete lacking in nothing. Therefore, God repurposes the initial trouble and trial to build a stronger believer. Just as going to the gym requires exerting yourself and straining your muscles, the results are a greater endurance and a stronger body. The spiritual discipline of prayer is that transformative exercise that produces spiritual transformation that allows one to count suffering as all joy.

Reflection Question

How can prayer help you have greater
endurance during your times of trouble?

DAY 20 | UNITED WE STAND, DIVIDED WE FALL

JOHN 17:20-23
Key Verses: 20-21

"I do not pray for these alone, but also for those who will believe in Me through their word; ²¹that they all may be one, as You, Father, are in Me, and I in You; that they also may be one in Us, that the world may believe that You sent Me.

Lions hunt in packs often with one lion appearing in plain sight before the herd of prey. The herd instantly and instinctively begins to run away in a panic only to discover that there are more lions to be encountered in their natural route of escape. A great planned confusion breaks out as the herd begins to dart in each direction seeking to avoid their would-be killers. Invariably the result is a separating of the herd with the young becoming separated from their parents. This was the design of the lions' strategy all along. The lions continue to catch and kill their prey not simply because of their strength and speed, but because of their strategy of divide and conquer. Satan, who the Bible refers to as a roaring lion, seeking whom he may devour, uses the same strategy of division. His goal is to divide marriages, families, churches, and believers from one another and ultimately from God.

One of the explicit prayers that Jesus lifted on our behalf was for our unity. The safety of the collective is stronger than we realize which is why the death of the unity of the herd always precedes the death of one of its members. We must remain constant in joining our prayer together with Jesus who prays that we remain one. The apostle Paul underscores the significance of unity in Ephesians when he says in 2:21 "in him the whole structure is joined together and grows into a holy temple in the Lord; in whom you are also built together spiritually into a dwelling place for God." Our prayer should focus not on divisions, but on the healing of divisions to maintain the strength of the herd.

I've had the privilege of going on safari in the beautiful Republic of South Africa which is really quite an exciting albeit harrowing experience. As you ride along in an open Jeep, the guide gives this simple instruction when approaching any animal including lions, "stay in the vehicle." The rationale comes next, *"the animals see us and the vehicle as one, and are scared to attack"*. If you leave the vehicle, you become an easy target. One of the things that we pray for the least, but should focus on the most is the necessity of unity. We were created to be in community together as believers and brothers and sisters in Christ Jesus.

Reflection Question

If there is division in your family, friendships or workplace, what are some ways you can help to restore unity?

DAY 21 | PARTING THE WAY FOR GOD'S PURPOSE

2 CORINTHIANS 6:14-17
Key Verse: 17

Therefore come out from them, and be separate from them, says the Lord, and touch nothing unclean; then I will welcome you, and I will be your father, and you shall be my sons and daughters, says the Lord Almighty.

Sifting is a major theme in the Kingdom of God. Sheep are divided from goats. The tares are allowed to grow among the wheat until ultimately they are separated after harvest. We are told that the wheat must be divided from the chaff. Therefore it should not come as an utter shock that Simon is informed that Satan has been granted permission to sift him. The key is to connect God's ultimate purpose of separation with Satan's immediate permission to separate. God desires His children to be unified one with another, but ultimately to be separated from unbelievers. Paul plainly states this principle of the church at Corinth, "come out from among them and be separate."

This concept is often taught in marriage classes as the "leave-cleave" principle. When God established the marriage between Adam and Eve, he gave this instruction, "therefore man shall leave his father and mother and cleave to his wife." Ultimately, we are only able to be fully unified when we have parted with those who are not of the same substance. Of course this is not a call to become spiritually elitist and separate ourselves based on a self-congratulatory perspective. Jesus spent much of his ministry decrying the Pharisees for doing just that. However, there are times when separation from the ungodly is vital to our growth and sometimes even our survival as believers. We must be careful that we do not hold on to these kinds of relationships out of insecurity, or desperation. This is why sometimes God must allow the adversary access to separate us because he knows that this is the only way we'll ever be divided from the chaff, tares, and the goats in our lives. Therefore we must pray for strength not to resuscitate those connections which God has allowed to die.

Reflection Question

What people or places is God separating you from?

Chapter Four:
THE POWER OF INTERCESSORY PRAYER

"but I have prayed for you"

DAY 22 | PRAYER IS SUFFICIENT

LUKE 22:31-34
Key Verse

"Simon, Simon, listen! Satan has demanded to sift all of you like wheat, but I have prayed for you that your own faith may not fail; and you, when once you have turned back, strengthen your brothers."

The idea of prayer being a sufficient remedy to whatever challenge we may face reminds me of a scene in one of my favorite movies, *Road House*. Patrick Swayze is playing the role of *'the cooler,'* the new head of security for a wild bar that attracts the wrong crowd and is nightly plagued with violence. Upon his arrival and introductions to the staff and other regulars, Swayze hears this common response: "I've heard of you, I thought that you would be bigger."

His first night on the job finds him involved in a fight where he has to disarm several bad guys, proving that his physical size was not a limitation on his ability to get the job done. I think sometimes we look at prayer as God's undersized answer to the tough issues that we must face. We think, "I've got real problems, and enemies." What is prayer in the face of such striking and intimidating opposition? The answer is simple: prayer is enough.

After alerting and informing Peter in no uncertain terms that Satan has been granted permission to place a target directly on Peter's back, Jesus then seeks to assure Peter by saying, "but I have prayed for you." Okay, full stop. Think about that for a minute. In the mind of Jesus, the peril that Peter and the disciples stand in, from an authorized demonic attack is alleviated because Jesus believes that prayer is enough to counteract the devil's plans. Jesus sees prayer as a sufficient remedy to the devil's plan to sift Peter and the disciples. Jesus demonstrates the primacy and power of intercessory prayer as a sufficient bulwark against demonic attack. Nothing additional to prayer is needed. His prayer is sufficient.

I had the privilege of attending NFL Hall of Fame Wide Receiver Jerry Rice's last home game with the San Francisco 49'ers. I was the guest of a friend who had a local radio sports show. We had passes to actually walk on the field as well as to be seated in the press box. The passes were fairly large, laminated red cards that we simply needed to display in order to gain access. There was no need for explanation of where we were going or demonstration of who we were. The passes were sufficient to give us full access. If we are to live a new life, we must see prayer as our all-access pass to God's throne. Prayer is enough.

Reflection Question
How much confidence do you have in the power of prayer?

DAY 23 | PRAYER IS YOUR ALL-ACCESS PASS TO GOD

COLOSSIANS 1:3-14
Key Verse: 9-11

"For this reason, since the day we heard it, we have not ceased praying for you and asking that you may be filled with the knowledge of God's will in all spiritual wisdom and understanding, ¹⁰so that you may lead lives worthy of the Lord, fully pleasing to him, as you bear fruit in every good work and as you grow in the knowledge of God"

If you were given access to have an audience with a powerful CEO or the President of the United States for ten minutes on any subject of your choosing, I suspect that you would want to make the most of that precious time. In knowing that the audience provides you with the opportunity to influence someone who is empowered to make real change, I bet you would carefully plan out your thoughts. Whenever we pray, we have an even greater opportunity because prayer gives us a private audience with the King of Kings and the Lord of Lords. It seems to me then that we should be intentional and prepared when we go to God in prayer.

Paul prayed with intentionality. He begins his letter to the believers in Colossae by telling them that he prays for them always and every day. He prays for them by name, and he prays for them by need. Often times our prayers are powerless because our prayers are purposeless. We have taken the time to call up heaven, where angels await to be dispatched to assist us and to dispense strength to undergird the causes of our hearts, only for us to wallow, meander, and drift from one thing to another without ever expressing a clear request or presenting a clear issue before the throne.

Our time in prayer is more fruitful when it is focused. Before praying, take the time to list your concerns: the needs of others, the fears that drain your enthusiasm, stubborn sins with which you struggle daily, and the names of people that burden your hurt. Actually, the formation of your prayer agenda is already a work of prayer. The Holy Spirit will reveal to you the things He would like to discuss with you. Then once you pray, and your mind begins to wander as all of ours do, you are able to re-center yourself and get back on track and make the most of the greatest audience that one can ever encounter – God.

What you will discover is that over time your prayer list will become the record of your testimony. You will find that as you make praying a daily habit, many things on your list will be resolved, yet not all in the manner that you requested. But you will begin to notice that as you've prayed about a particular issue, you will be in a better position to celebrate your victories or to heal from your disappointments. Just as most word-processing software allows us to "track" the changes that we've made to a document, so will your prayer journal allow you to track the changes that the Lord makes in your life and in the lives of those whom you have covered in prayer.

Reflection Question

As you pray with intentionality, what concerns will you take to God?

DAY 24 | PRAY FOR ME AND I'LL PRAY FOR YOU

ACTS 12:1-11
Key Verse: 5
While Peter was kept in prison, the church prayed fervently to God for him.

One of the most concerning trends of the day in which we live is the cultural shifts in America and around the world towards individualism. More and more we find ourselves relying on others less and less. As a consequence, this independent orientation makes us less likely to seek assistance whether it is spiritual, relational or professional. Christianity is not designed to be practiced alone in a corner, but in a community of faith where we may pray for one another. The truth is sometimes our faith is shattered, we are simply too weak emotionally, or we are so conflicted in our thinking that our prayer life dries up. While we are called to soldier through, we must recognize that God has already provided for these dry and difficult seasons of our lives. Intercessory prayer is needed because sometimes we feel unable to pray for ourselves.

When parts of municipal electrical grids go down, those who manage them are able to shift power from other places so that the entire area may continue to function. When we pray for one another we truly are able to shift spiritual power from one place to another to provide spiritual support for the brokenness of a particular person. In Acts 12 we are given a portrait of the power of intercessory prayer. While James' blood still hardens on the ground from being beheaded, Herod promises to do the same thing to Peter on the following day, and then sends Peter to his jail cell. While Peter is locked up for what should be his last night on earth, we are told that the church prayed hard for Peter. Their prayer in verse five precedes the appearance of the angel in verse seven, which leads to Peter's release from his restraints and confinement behind prison doors and gates.

Who has benefited from your prayer life? Just as Peter would always be thankful to God for delivering him from his prison cell, and certain death, he would always hold dear those believers who interceded in prayer on his behalf. There should be someone who can associate her blessing with your prayer life. Of course, all glory and credit belongs to God, but there should be an honorable mention for going to the throne of grace on someone's behalf.

Reflection Question

Think about the collective prayers of others from whom you have benefited. Who is God asking you to intercede for in prayer today?

DAY 25 | GOD HEARS AND RESPONDS TO OUR PRAYERS

NUMBERS 14:1-39
Key Verse: 19

Pardon the iniquity of this people, I pray, according to the greatness of Your mercy, just as You have forgiven this people, from Egypt even until now.

After God delivered the children of Israel out of Egypt and into the wilderness on the way to the Promised Land, they began to complain against God and long for the fleshpots of Egypt. The depth of this insult, after having prayed to God to deliver them from Egypt, was so great that God's righteous indignation was kindled so that he declared that he would destroy them and detailed how he would go about doing so. Yet Moses interceded on behalf of the people, and begged God for mercy on behalf of a people who deserved none. And amazingly, God altered His plans, sentencing those of Moses' generation to die in the wilderness over a 40-year period, and only allowing Joshua and Caleb to enter into the Promised Land with the next generation.

So powerful is intercessory prayer that it can literally change the mind of God. This of course is so awesome a claim that our minds almost reject it instantly. How can a God who is sovereign be influenced by a mere mortal? This is not a difficult concept for any parent to understand. Raising children is a series of harsh stands and hasty retreats. My wife and I decided that we needed to keep our daughter from sneaking into our bed in the middle of the night. Yet each night she somehow ends up there. It's easy to say that we're both too tired to put her back in her bed, but the truth is that our harsh stand melts into a hasty retreat in the face of our daughter, with her arms outstretched, asking to be picked up so that she can be near us. Our ceaseless love for her overrides our stand, even though it is right, with a mercy that draws her closer to us. This is not a challenge to our authority but a demonstration of it. If God cannot change His mind, it would be a limitation on God's sovereignty. The fact that God's love for us can override His requirement for judgment is a demonstration of His endless and unequalled love for us.

We must pray to God with an unrelenting posture to push past the perceived no's in order to get to the heart of the yes's that God wants us to have. God longs for us to have so much confidence in Him, love for Him, and boldness with Him, that He is able to reverse Himself and draw us ever closer.

Reflection Question

*How has your intercessory prayer influenced
God's decision on a particular matter?*

DAY 26 | JESUS PRAYS ON OUR BEHALF

ROMANS 8:31-34
Key Verse: 34

Who is he who condemns? It is Christ who died, and furthermore is also risen, who is even at the right hand of God, who also makes intercession for us.

One of the most profound realizations of knowing Jesus is how clear an example he provides for us so that we might learn to live victoriously. Jesus, throughout the scriptures, regularly attends corporate worship, pays tithes and taxes, and prays for himself and for others. One would think that as the son of God, Jesus would be exempt from such elementary practices in the same way that there are many tasks beneath the CEO of a company or a 5-star general in the United States Army. Yet, the scriptures make it clear that Jesus did not just preach a prayerful lifestyle but he practiced it as a necessary means of his own spiritual journey. If Jesus who walked on water, healed the sick, and raised the dead still needed to pray, we should expect nothing less in our need to be in daily prayer.

While Jesus was on earth he prayed for us, so that we know how he prays for us in glory. Jesus prays a prayer of intercession for us at the right hand of God the father. This is the great truth that Paul gives us to know in Romans 8:34. Jesus' role as an advocate or helper, allows him to petition God on our behalf. Not only does Jesus intercede for us, but so does the Holy Spirit. Romans 8:26-27 says, *Likewise the Spirit also helps in our weaknesses. For we do not know what we should pray for as we ought, but the Spirit Himself makes intercession for us with groanings which cannot be uttered. ²⁷Now He who searches the hearts knows what the mind of the Spirit is, because He makes intercession for the saints according to the will of God."* Literally, the Holy Spirit interprets our prayers while intuiting the mind of the Father so that our prayers come into line with God's will.

It is powerful to consider that intercessory prayer is not merely a practice that believers should exercise amongst themselves, but it is a practice that God engages himself. Both the Holy Spirit and Jesus intercede on our behalf. Neither the Holy Spirit nor Jesus are praying for themselves – they are praying for us, interceding on our behalf.

Intercessory prayer is so important that God not only endorses it for us but He exercises it as well. What a great revelation! While we pray, God is praying for us. Therefore the working of prayer itself is not only about the individual talking to God, but simultaneously, God talking to Himself about us. Since we don't know what to pray the Holy Spirit edits our prayer, and through Jesus, shares it with the Father. As we pray we are able to listen in on this Trinitarian conversation (God, Jesus and the Holy Spirit) which then becomes the revelation of God's will for our lives. God's voice in prayer is the holy eavesdropping that we are allowed to listen in on. What a sacred privilege it is to listen in on heavenly chatter on our behalf. Prayer belongs to God, is inhabited by God, and is given to us as a gift. Therefore we are blessed with the presence of God in the process of God interceding on our behalf in the very moment of our prayer.

Reflection Question

How does it feel knowing that God is praying for you?

DAY 27 | PRAYERS OF INTERCESSION FOR ONE ANOTHER

JAMES 5:13-19
Key Verse: 14

Is anyone among you sick? Let him call for the elders of the church, and let them pray over him, anointing him with oil in the name of the Lord. [15]And the prayer of faith will save the sick, and the Lord will raise him up. And if he has committed sins, he will be forgiven.

From time to time we hear happy instances of people "paying it forward." It often involves someone in Starbucks paying for the person behind them, with the recipient then responding by doing the same. It has been reported that these runs of generosity focusing on others sometimes last for hours and involve hundreds of people. I believe that the logic of the action unlocks the true desire of the human spirit. When we are given something with no strings attached, with no sense of obligation to do anything, we tend to feel free to do what makes us feel the best - giving to someone else. If you have been a beneficiary of intercessory prayer, it is time that you become a benefactor.

In Luke 22, Jesus informs Peter that he has been engaged in intercessory prayer on his behalf. James informs us that one of our primary responsibilities is to pray for others - to petition God on behalf of individuals who are suffering, sick, or who have confessed their sin. James uses the term *the prayer of faith*, which is not a specific set of words, but prayer characterized by its expectation to transform the life of the individual who is being lifted up to God.

Most importantly, this passage in James provides us a clear image of what the Christian life looks like. It is not individualistic. It occurs in relationship with other people of faith. It is not self-centered but considers and acts toward the needs of others. It is not self-rationalizing, but requires us to confess our sins and shortcomings to others who do not judge us, but pray for our recovery and restoration. In other words, intercessory prayer is necessary for a healthy Christian community. While all of us should have alone time with God, none of us should live pulled away from other believers. Prayer is not a single rope from earth to heaven. It is a network of individuals, who are connected to God and to one another in a way that brings transformation, healing, and wholeness.

The almost invisible strings of a web are able to withstand pressures well beyond their individual capacity because of the way they are networked together. The configuration is not a matter of artistic design, but rather architectural planning. The web is spun, cross-bracing and networked in such a way that it can achieve its purpose. Likewise when believers come together, a web of faith should be created spiritually with the strong bearing the infirmities of the weak, with each one seeking to outdo the other in showing honor, and most of all, praying in faith for the blessing of one's brother or sister in Christ.

Just as the web is not randomly assembled, but intentionally assembled, so also should there be a sense of order and deliberate effort given toward creating and sustaining the bond of faith. Intercessory prayer serves as both the string and the pattern that holds the community of faith together.

Reflection Question
Are you part of a spiritual network?

DAY 28 | PRAY FOR YOUR ENEMIES

LUKE 23:33-38
Key Verse: 34

Then Jesus said, "Father, forgive them, for they do not know what they do." And they divided His garments and cast lots.

Before we got our dog, Huck, I was always pretty cynical about the term "man's best friend." It seemed strange to me that an animal would be held in such high esteem. Now I get it. Huck is happiest when he is nestled up with his pack, which is our family. Literally, when we embrace one another, it is normal for him to come and lean up against us or place his head in our laps while we watch television.

One of his most endearing traits is his protective nature. Huck is a watch dog who takes his responsibilities seriously. When we go to sleep at night, he does not sleep next to our bed. Instead, he positions himself in front of the door to our room. It is as if he is saying that anyone or anything that seeks to do my pack any kind of harm must first come through me. If Huck hears a bump in the night, he instantly goes to investigate it, growling and barking to indicate his intentions. The best part about Huck is that we never had to train him to do any of this. This is because his breed has been engineered to be watchful. His behavior is simply second nature.

One of the signs of your maturity as a believer is when you become watchful. You discover within yourself an intense protective sensitivity to the needs of others. One of the key ways that this trait presents itself is through intercessory prayer. Just like Huck, you instinctively position yourself between your pack and any impending danger when you pray for people that are in need. This is exactly what Jesus does for all of humanity as he is crucified at Calvary. His prayer, *"Father forgive them for they know not what they do,"* is an intense plea on behalf of not just those who are physically facilitating his torture, but for all of humanity, those who are spiritually participating with his crucifixion as all of our sins are transferred upon Jesus.

This prayer from Jesus is designed to get in between the sinful man that should be punished and the righteous judgment of God. Often times we are called to pray not for the innocent but for the guilty. We are called to intercede on behalf of people who have brazenly sinned against others and against God. We need not shrink back from this responsibility. In fact, we are being Christ-like when we position ourselves to protect our pack. Here's the rub – as believers we are even called to see our enemies as our pack and to pray for them as well. Jesus admonishes us to do just that in Luke 6:27-28 when he says, *"But I say unto you which hear, love your enemies, do good to them which hate you, bless them that curse you and pray for them which despitefully use you."* To pray for those who attack you and are against you is counter-intuitive to our nature, but it is a breed standard of a true disciple and evidence of your growth in God.

Reflection Question

What will it take for you to pray on behalf of those who are not a part of your pack?

Chapter Five:
PRAYING FOR FAITH

"that your own faith may not fail"

DAY 29 | PROTECTING YOUR FAITH

LUKE 22:31-34
Key Verse: 31-32

"Simon, Simon, listen! Satan has demanded to sift all of you like wheat, but I have prayed for you that your own faith may not fail; and you, when once you have turned back, strengthen your brothers."

Whether one is talking about the patents owned by a technology company, the launch codes held within a military unit or the state secrets of a government – it is important to protect one's most important and valuable assets. The most important asset that any human can possess is faith in God. Jesus' concern about Peter's faith reveals its primacy in his life and the life of every person. Jesus is not concerned about Peter's reputation or emotional disappointment, but about his *faith* - which underscores its necessity to ultimate victory. If Jesus' primary concern for Peter, who has been designated as the rock of the church, is the strength of his faith, then it appears that you and I should more closely guard our faith and nurture it. The truth is, though, most of us do not properly value the significance of our faith primarily because we were never taught that it is priceless.

How many collectibles worth millions of dollars have been either sold for spare change, neglected until the point of their ruin, or worse – just thrown away? In each case, the loss of the collectible was due to the ignorance of the owner. In each instance the only hope for the collectible (and the owner) is that someone with greater understanding would share with her the true value of what is owned. Let this sentence be a permanent and constant reminder for you of the most important thing in your life – *it is faith in God.*

Once you know what is most important, the second most important thing is what secures it. According to Jesus' message to Peter, prayer is *the thing* that sustains and secures faith. A key without proper placement in the lock and the torque necessary to turn It results in a locked door. It has been rightly said that faith is the key and prayer unlocks the door. Therefore, we must not simply pray in faith, but we must pray that our faith will not fail.

Jesus has already declared that Peter will be the rock of the church. Here Jesus tells us that the core of this rock is Peter's faith. Whatever we seek to accomplish personally, professionally, or spiritually will always be determined by the strength of our faith. Attending to the strength of our faith is the power of our prayer life. It is in prayer that our resolve is renewed, courage is crystallized, and God's vision for our lives comes into view.

Reflection Question

Knowing that faith in God is your most valuable possession, how will you safeguard it?

DAY 30 | Praying for Faith

MARK 9:14-29
Key Verse: 21
Immediately the father of the child
cried out and said with tears, "Lord, I
believe; help my unbelief!"

As believers, it is not enough for us to pray *in faith*, but we must pray *for faith*. Faith is trust in God despite the difficulty of the circumstances. Certainly in this passage, this father has reason to be skeptical about Jesus' power to deliver his son from demonic attack. After all, this demon has literally vexed his son all of his life, often throwing him into the fire and water and boldly vexing him in Jesus' presence. The man is still emotionally reeling from the disciples' failure to exorcise this demon from his child. Undoubtedly, this is only the latest attempt that this man has made to see his son freed and delivered. He has faith, but his faith is being stymied by deep and multiple long-term disappointments.

If we are honest with ourselves, we must acknowledge that we don't always have great faith, mountain-moving faith, or even pure faith. While great faith is both admirable and attainable, we must know what to do when our faith is weak and worn down.

Often our faith is pock-marked and riddled with holes having been dragged through the turmoil and disappointments of life. It is then that we must ask for faith in prayer. I know that seems odd theologically so consider this practically. When I was a child, my first grade class was given the opportunity to buy small gifts for our respective families in the weeks leading up to Christmas. Rhinestone rings for Mom and a shiny pen for Dad. Nothing was more than a few dollars. The point of the exercise was to get us to think beyond ourselves. Even at these low, low prices most kids were still put in the position of having to solicit their parents for money to buy the gifts. Despite the fact that my parents paid for their own gifts, it did not lessen the pride that I had in giving them their gifts, nor their pleasure in receiving them. This is how it works with faith with our Heavenly Father. God's word is clear that without faith it is impossible to please Him, but God's word also makes clear that He freely gives to each of us a measure of faith. Therefore, the faith that we need to please God comes from God. We should never be bashful about admitting our lack of faith or asking for more faith.

Of all the legitimate requests that we can make of God, whether it is healing for ourselves or others, the forgiveness of sins, or the restoration of a significant relationship, God takes special joy in receiving requests for faith. Jesus' strong response in the passage to this father's questioning of his ability to do "anything," causes the man to acknowledge the weakness of his faith and to then request more faith. "*I believe, help my unbelief.*"

In the same way that teachers must strongly confront their students in order for them to learn and grow, Jesus' challenge, though at first glance seemingly insensitive, is understood as the height of compassion. The truth is that when our faith is weak it may seem that God is being cold or cruel in not coddling us in our misery; however, it is sometimes God's challenges that ignite our greatest leaps of faith.

Reflection Question

Have you ever considered that by simply acknowledging your doubts about God to God, you will be offering God an invitation to strengthen your faith?

DAY 31 | WITHOUT FAITH IT IS IMPOSSIBLE TO PLEASE GOD

Key Verse: HEBREWS 11:6

And without faith it is impossible to please God, for whoever would approach him must believe that he exists and that he rewards those who seek him.

Last Christmas our daughter became frustrated after unwrapping the present that she had requested, a toy that she had seen advertised for months. She tore open the packaging and became upset that the toy wouldn't function. She was crestfallen and confused as she was certain that this toy was broken. It was then that I said to her, "there is nothing wrong with it darling. It just needs batteries." After I installed the batteries, the toy functioned flawlessly and continued to do so until those batteries ran down.

Just as batteries powered the toy, faith powers the believer. Biblical knowledge cannot power it. Church attendance cannot do it. Even being a good person cannot replace the primary function of faith in establishing and developing our relationship with God. In fact, without faith we can have no relationship with God, not to mention even please God. Faith is the foundation upon which the entirety of one's new life in Christ is built. We are saved by our faith in the finished work of Jesus on the Cross. Faith is the means by which we hold that God exists, and that He rewards those who diligently seek Him. Prayer is the fundamental way that we seek Him. Therefore when we pray in faith we are assured of God's reward which is His presence.

Once I calmed our daughter's frustration and placed the batteries in the toy, she happily played with her new toy. It was a loud and active toy much to the chagrin of her parents who were seeking a quiet home. Even so, our daughter played with her toy and all was well – that is, until a few days later when the batteries had worn down. Our daughter was confused because she did not understand that batteries can lose their power. We had to teach her that those batteries needed to be removed and recharged.

This is how faith and prayer work together. As we pray we are recharged. We have faith and we are inspired to pray and lay claim to God's promises. As life happens to us in big and small ways, we will find ourselves being drained of our energy and enthusiasm. We must recognize that prayer increases faith and faith empowers our prayer life. Through the spiritual residue of our prayer life we receive the power to live victoriously.

Reflection Question

What issues are draining your energy that require you to have greater faith to conquer?

#ignite50Day31

DAY 32 | DISTINCTIVE FAITH

LUKE 7:1-10
Key Verse: 9

When Jesus heard this he was amazed at him, and turning to the crowd that followed him, he said, "I tell you, not even in Israel have I found such faith."

We live in a world of personalization. We can custom-order our coffee, our clothes, our homes and almost any other thing imaginable. In such a tailored world it is easy to begin to believe that life is meant to accommodate itself to our desires. The reality is that while retail has embraced customization, life has not. There are hard truths in life that are immune to our preferences. Not only do we not get to pick our families, our health conditions, our gender, or our race – we also do not get to choose what moves the heart of God. Nothing moves God's heart like faith. This is quite evident in this text in Luke where we see Jesus in a state of awe.

After the centurion has made his request of Jesus to heal his servant, Jesus – out of compassion – is ready to comply by going to the man's house to perform the miracle. The centurion assures Jesus that such extraordinary efforts will not be necessary because he understands the fundamental nature of authority as the ability to simply command things to happen at which point there can be nothing but compliance. It is important to note that the centurion is not teaching Jesus. Obviously, the Lord is aware of his own power. Rather, Jesus had become accustomed to the low-levels of faith of the people in this region.

What made Jesus marvel was the maturity and strength of this centurion's faith which was unique from the basic and weak level of those in Israel. In other words, his faith was outstanding.

I wonder how much our faith weighs on God's heart. Is it so light that it is almost imperceptible, requiring God to provide direct involvement, signs and wonders to assure us of his power? Or is our faith so substantial that it gets God's attention because it is so sound and solid? The weight of our prayer life is measured in units of faith. Our aim should be rather than having little faith to instead be found having great faith or outstanding faith.

In the weight-conscious culture today, many people regularly monitor their weight with sophisticated scales. It is commonly understood that the two greatest factors that affect our weight are diet and exercise. Our choices concerning what we eat and whether or not we workout will be revealed at the scale. As believers, our weight is dictated by how much of the word we consume and how many times we exercise our faith through prayer.

Reflection Question

*Is your faith out of shape or is it maintaining
a healthy diet of "prayer"?*

DAY 33 | SPECIFYING THE OBJECT OF YOUR FAITH

ACTS 3:1-10
Key Verse: 2

And a certain man lame from his mother's womb was carried, whom they laid daily at the gate of the temple which is called Beautiful, to ask alms from those who entered the temple;

The key to our prayer lives is to be willing to identify and address our core issues with God. Years ago, I coughed while speaking to a friend who quickly inquired as to what I was doing to address my cold. I told her that I was eating cough drops and drinking tea with honey. She laughed and then said something that I'll never forget. She said, *"Well, I guess that's alright if your goal is to just treat the symptoms."* It was at this point that I remembered that she had a Ph.D. in Public Health. She went on to point out that the cough drops and tea would make my symptoms more tolerable, but would not address my actual sickness.

I believe that most of us pray to God in the same way. Rather than seeking relief for the core issues of fears, brokenness, or loneliness or grief - we simply pray for cough drops and tea. We ask God for superficial things that will make our fears and hurts more tolerable. When Jesus prayed for Peter's faith, he was addressing his core issue.

In Acts 3 the lame man by the Beautiful Gate begs for money every day so that he can return the next day to beg some more. Generally this is the same way that most of us pray to God. We simply ask for just enough to make it one more step, rather than asking God to deal with our core issues. The man's core issue was his physical disability, which resulted in his poor financial position, yet his request of Peter and John was not for healing, but for money to make it another day. Of course it doesn't make sense to ask something of someone that they do not possess. The regular crowd that passed by this man at the Beautiful Gate could only offer him money but Peter and John could offer more.

The Bible says that when Peter and John approached him, Peter looked intently at him. Peter's gaze looks past the man's financial request and sees his real need for healing. Jesus said *"ask and you shall receive, seek and you shall find, knock and the door will be opened to you."* Honestly identifying the real object of your prayer allows you to ask, seek, and knock for the right thing. One of the joys of a vibrant prayer life is that God reveals the real roots of the issues with which we struggle, yet knowing the root cause does not by itself bring resolution. We must then choose either to address it or avoid it.

Reflection Question

Are you praying to God about your core issues or just what you think you need in order to make it to the next step?

DAY 34 | FAITH EXPECTATION

1 KINGS 18: 41-46
Key Verses: 42-43

So Ahab went up to eat and drink. And Elijah went up to the top of Carmel; then he bowed down on the ground, and put his face between his knees, [43]and said to his servant, "Go up now, look toward the sea." So he went up and looked, and said, "There is nothing." And seven times he said, "Go again."

After Elijah heard in his spirit the sound of the abundance of rain pouring after a three-year drought, he went with his servant to Mount Carmel to pray. After his first prayer, his servant saw no sign of rain so Elijah prayed again and again. Ultimately, after his seventh time of praying, a cloud the size of man's hand appeared. Elijah and his servant hastily moved because he knew that this great rain was now coming and he did not want to be overtaken by it. Elijah's belief in the power of prayer is what caused him to pray repeatedly and to not become discouraged or give up.

Likewise, when we pray we should rise from our knees expecting to see something different than what we saw before we knelt down. Our prayer life must be rooted in faith and we must see prayer as a means by which to reach God and to see God move in our lives. Therefore, prayer cannot be something done out of duty, out of obligation or religious routine. Prayer must be viewed as effective by the one who is praying. When there are emergencies we understand that our first response should be to call for emergency services by dialing 911. Our expectation is that at the conclusion of our call, there should be the sound of sirens in the distance, the appearance of flashing lights, and finally the arrival of responders to favorably impact the outcome of events already in progress. This is the kind of expectation that should be tied to our prayer life. Even if we have to spiritually dial 911 several times until we see a sign that a shift is occurring, we should be confident in our prayers.

An oft missed aspect of an effective prayer life is not simply our confidence in God, but also our confidence in our cause. As Elijah prayed, he did so knowing that God had already placed in his spirit the urge to pray for rain. Notice that just because God desires something for us and reveals it to us, it does not negate our need to ask for it in faith. What it does do is embolden us to know that we are making a request that will be granted.

Charitable foundations operate in this way. They must spend money to advertise the fact that they desire to give money to certain causes. They will even contact non-profit organizations that they would like to fund, yet that non-profit must still complete an application and meet the requirements of the foundation in order to receive the financial reward. The non-profit is happy to comply with the process because it is confident that it will receive what it needs and what has been promised to it. Likewise, this is the surety with which we approach God's throne – knowing that we are asking things that are according to His will.

Reflection Question

When you pray do you believe you are praying according to God's will or do you get discouraged when you don't see anything happening right away?

Chapter Six:
The Role of Repentance and Redemption in Prayer

"and you, when you have turned back..."

DAY 35 | FALLING FOR YOUR FAITH

LUKE 22:31-32
Key Verse: 31-32

And the Lord said, "Simon, Simon! Indeed, Satan has asked for you, that he may sift you as wheat. But I have prayed for you, that your faith should not fail; and when you have returned to Me, strengthen your brethren."

In this passage, Jesus' presumption is laid bare – that despite his prayer Peter will falter in his faith and fall, but that he will survive the fall. Later on Jesus will explicitly inform Peter that he will deny him three times. These words must have been emotionally difficult for Peter to understand. Peter felt his love and loyalty towards Jesus were unshakeable, yet he is told that he will still fall.

Richard Rohr, a contemporary theologian and best-selling author, would suggest that rather than falling down Peter is in fact falling upward. In his 2011 book, *Falling Upward*, Rohr says this: "We are not helping our children by always preventing them from what might be necessary falling, because you learn how to recover from falling, by falling!" [1]Central to the Christian life is this notion of redemption. It is as obvious as the significance of Easter and as available as our next prayer. When we pray we are joined by faith through the Holy Spirit to the same power that raised Jesus from the dead – a power which can help us to get up from wherever we have fallen.

Like millions of football fans, I enjoy watching the NFL behind-the-scenes show *Hard Knocks*. By allowing cameras unfettered access to the training camp process, practices, the locker room, and even the interaction at the hotel, the producers allow viewers to get a real sense of what a different environment professional football players must learn to navigate.

[1]Richard Rohr, *Falling Upward: A Spirituality for the Two Halves of Life*, (San Francisco: Jossey-Bass, 2011). 28

Each show concludes with its own intrigue as the issue of who will be cut from the team is pressed more and more. Each player whose future is uncertain is constantly looking for signs that his position is secure.

In one instance, while discussing a defensive scheme, the coach remarked about how this approach was going to work very well for the player against a specific team. The assumption of the coach was that the player would be around, which gave great relief to the player. His assumption was really an announcement that *"you're going to make the team."* Jesus' prediction to Peter, *"when you have turned back"* is really a pronouncement that repentance will happen for you, which means your worst faith chapter will not be your last faith chapter. Through prayer we are able to pick up on little hints and glimpses of ourselves in the mind of God. Rather than simply giving us confirmation that we'll make it through a season of struggle, God will show us his vision for us in the future, which implies not only our future success but our present survival.

When we disappoint ourselves and disappoint God, we find courage in knowing that we will be restored. This great assurance is good to know in our heads, but it is more important to receive it in our hearts. Our prayers of repentance and requests for redemption do the lion share of the work in helping to know that God has forgiven us. Like watching an action movie in which the hero finds herself trapped, cornered, outnumbered and wounded, in the moment we may feel the same way, believing that there is no escape route.

The truth is, if we step back from the moment, we'll realize that without the hero, the movie cannot continue. This quick resetting of the way that we are viewing the movie instantly gives us relief. Our prayers relieve us of our anxieties and restore our assurance that our failures are not final.

Reflection Question

What glimpses of the future are you seeing from God when you pray, even when it's hard to see beyond the moment?

DAY 36 | SERVING GOD AFTER YOU HAVE FALLEN—LIFE AFTER THE FALL

LUKE 36:36-50 #7
Key Verse: 47

Therefore I say to you, her sins, which are many, are forgiven, for she loved much. But to whom little is forgiven, the same loves little.

One of the amazing features of the human body is its ability to produce and retain antibodies in response to certain kinds of infections. Immediately, the infection may cause the individual all kinds of discomfort and pain. However, as the body reacts to combat this attack by producing antibodies, this new code is stored in the body. If the same or similar infection occurs in the future, the body now has a proven formula to repel it. In actuality the body has a greater capacity post-attack, than prior to the infection. Likewise, whenever we endure a crisis of faith where we have responded by either turning toward sin or displaying an attitude of a lack of trust in God, what we find is that on the other side of our crisis our faith is put back together better than it was before. These circumstances have a way of humbling us, making us more conscious of God's love and grace in our lives. This produces in us a greater desire to worship, to serve and to love.

As Jesus shared this parable about two persons being forgiven of their debts, with the greater debtor being naturally more appreciative, he crystalized his point saying, "the one to whom little is forgiven, loves little." Jesus' statement suggests that in falling down, we appreciate more fully that God has to stoop to pick us up (an understanding not readily obvious to those who see themselves as living upright). Our confession of our sin stirs the spiritual sediment of humility within our souls.

A part of the Methodist Holy Communion liturgy is "The prayer of Humiliation." To the modern reader, this seems very odd and off-putting because we tend to think of humiliation as a negative and painful experience caused by someone who has wronged us in an embarrassing way. However, humiliation really is the act of simply being humble. As we consider the severity and frequency of our sins, we – like the much-forgiven debtor – are overwhelmed with a sense of appreciation. This powerful emotion ignites our prayer life. We may be moved to tears or we may be overcome with amazement in understanding the depth of God's love for us.

When we pray it becomes passionate and powerful. If our prayers remain merely as exercises of our minds, then they have no access to minister to our hearts and souls. The great realization is that forgiveness unlocks the whole of the believer to be enraptured in this moment of prayer. The net result then is a believer who is closer to God, stronger in faith and less prone to stray than was true before the fall.

Reflection Question

What impact has prayer had in helping you to recuperate from a crisis, allowing you to see God's sanctifying grace at work?

#ignite50Day36

DAY 37 | THE DIFFERENCE BETWEEN SIMON AND JUDAS

MATTHEW 26:69-75
Key Verse: 75

And Peter remembered the word of Jesus who had said to him, "Before the rooster crows, you will deny Me three times." So he went out and wept bitterly.

Key Verse: Matthew 27:5

Then he threw down the pieces of silver in the temple and departed, and went and hanged himself.

Of the twelve disciples both Peter and Judas stand out in their betrayals of Jesus at his final hour. Judas betrayed Jesus by literally selling him out for 30 pieces of silver. This fact is so startling because it points to the pre-conceived arrangement and intentionality that motivated Judas to act. On the other hand, Peter had proclaimed himself a cut above the other disciples declaring that while the rest would be betray Jesus, he would be with Jesus.

Peter's betrayal was also startling as it came in phases with him having denied Christ three times. While the severity of each man's betrayal far surpassed the other disciples, here is where the similarities end. For Judas, after he committed his act of betrayal, he went out at night and hanged himself. Peter did not take such a terrible recourse. Instead of taking his life, he simply returned to his former life of fishing when Jesus appeared. Peter led the charge to be reconciled with Christ and ultimately to establish the church.

The difference in these two men was that one saw life after the fall and the other did not. No matter how far or how often we betray our relationship with Christ, we are assured by the demonstration of his love for us at Calvary that there is always life after the fall. If the most difficult act for Jesus was to purchase our forgiveness with his blood, then the most difficult act for us is to accept his forgiveness and to forgive ourselves. Jesus' words to Peter not only inform him of demonic attacks, but also assure him of his survival and restoration. Prayer is designed to close the distance between us and God caused by our betrayals and to bring us back into right relationship with God so that we never will even consider or resort to suicidal habits or behaviors like Judas. Instead we will be restored like Peter and reconciled back to Christ through his unwavering and unfailing love.

Recovery from sin is often like recovery from a major physical injury. There is the physiological side of things – the mending of tendons and reduction of swelling. Equally important is the mental, emotional and spiritual state of the patient. Often it is the belief in one's ability to recover that enables some patients to achieve a much higher state of health than others with similar conditions. Likewise as believers, we must recognize that the forgiveness of sins has been accomplished by Jesus' completed work on the Cross. What allows one believer to be restored after sin while others wallow or even wither away in sin, is the belief that one can recover and truly be restored. We must, therefore, pray for faith that will facilitate our full recovery and restoration in God.

Reflection Question

What is keeping you from being in a close relationship with God?

DAY 38 | PRODIGAL SON

LUKE 15:11-24
Key Verse: 18-19

I will arise and go to my father, and will say to him,
"Father, I have sinned against heaven and before you,
¹⁹and I am no longer worthy to be called your son.
Make me like one of your hired servants."

Years ago I had the opportunity to go horseback riding with a colleague who had his own ranch in North Carolina. Since I was a novice, he picked a horse that was of good temperament, saddled it, and then led it into a fence that had been made into a circle. There he ran the horse at good pace for about five to seven minutes. When he was finished, the horse was panting and sweat had already beaded up on its face. He then brought the horse over to me and told me to get on. As I inquired as to what all of the business was about with the horse running in a circle, he explained it this way. "I had to take some of the strength off of him." He said "if you had tried to ride him without the time in the circle he would have been more apt to resist you, and possibly even throw you. But now that he's been broken down a little he'll follow wherever you lead him."

Given our rebellious nature, every now and then God has to allow us to experience the hardships born out of our own hard-heartedness until finally we've been broken down to the point where we'll follow God. That is what the story of the prodigal son means to me. A young man who thought he could live life by his own rules, until he hit rock bottom in a hog pen, became repentant and returned to his father. Of course, the beauty of the story was that rather than rejecting him, his father readily received him. When we pray authentically, we not only can acknowledge our mistakes, but now that we've been broken, we can take confidence in knowing that our Heavenly Father stands with arms open to welcome us back into right relationship.

When we are too head-strong, we make ourselves unavailable to God's power because God resists the proud, but He gives grace to the humble (James 4:6). But, having to go through bitter and difficult times is not the only path that leads to brokenness. Rather than having to be humbled by the hot walking processes of life, we can simply choose to humble ourselves in prayer. Prayer brings us to a place of a broken spirit and contrite heart that God requires of us as written in Psalm 51. When we are at this place before God, it makes prayer a much less painful process for us.

In other words, we may choose to fall on our knees in prayer or we may be knocked to our knees by life. While both achieve the same result, from my experience I recommend the former.

Reflection Question

What things, habits or behavior do you need to release and fall to your knees in order to be welcomed back into God's forgiving arms?

DAY 39 | ACCEPTING GOD'S GRACE

PHILIPPIANS 3:12-16
Key Verse: 13-14

Brethren, I do not count myself to have apprehended; but one thing I do, forgetting those things which are behind and reaching forward to those things which are ahead, [14]I press toward the goal for the prize of the upward call of God in Christ Jesus.

One of the many attributes ascribed in scripture to Satan is being "the accuser of the brothers." The way I think about it is that Satan constructs a huge movie screen in our minds that constantly plays a movie of all of our worst moments like times when we allowed our anger to say and do hurtful things; times when we disgraced God, our families, and ourselves by our sinful actions; or even times when we quietly told God no to satisfy our own desires. Satan understands that the more he can turn our focus on our mistakes, the less we will feel worthy of being in a thriving relationship with the God that we have sinned against and disappointed.

But as believers saved by the blood of Jesus, we must hold on to this one truth. God is over it, passed it, and He's not even remembering it any longer. God has forgiven us, so we must forgive ourselves. To truly forgive ourselves we must have faith that we cannot fall lower than God's grace. We must confess our sins to God, and to fellow believers, and we must pray that the Holy Spirit would take down the big screen that keeps playing our worst moments. This taking down is generally not a one-time thing. We must allow the Holy Spirit to remind us and assure us of God's forgiveness over and over again.

As we pray in the Spirit we are assured of God's boundless love for us and His forgiveness. Even more, God replaces the regrets of seeing the mistakes of our past with the joy of seeing His plans and promises for our future. Forgiveness leads to new vision which leads to new life. Just as you cannot drive forward safely for long with your eyes affixed to the rearview mirror, we cannot move forward in our spiritual walk stuck on what we did in the past

God invites us, through Paul's words to the church at Philippi, to forget those things which are behind and to instead strain toward what lies ahead. We are called to press toward the mark of the high calling of Christ Jesus. Notice the effort implied in the process of moving forward. Forgetting, straining and pressing imply great exertion. That is because it is not natural to distance one's self from one's experience and to then launch one's self into a different reality. In fact, without the power of prayer at work to grant strength for our weaknesses in our attempts to move forward, we will find ourselves both fixed and frustrated in our current state.

Whether our past includes abuse, betrayal, or gross suffering, it is quite natural to hold on to these realities rather than to move forward. Therefore, we need the power of God that is accessible through prayer, to aid us in doing supernaturally what cannot be done naturally – and that is, forgetting, straining and pressing forward.

Reflection Question

What "movie screen moments" of your past are causing you to have difficulties accepting God's grace?

DAY 40 | REPENT FOR THE KINGDOM OF GOD

MARK 1:14-15
Key Verse: **14-15**

Now after John was put in prison, Jesus came to Galilee, preaching the gospel of the kingdom of God, ¹⁵and saying, "The time is fulfilled, and the kingdom of God is at hand. Repent, and believe in the gospel."

Once in a while when I am being guided by my navigation system it advises me to take a turn that I think is unwise. My response generally is to comply but every now and again, I choose to chart my own path. Something tells me that my path will be shorter or more scenic. So, off I go. The voice of the navigation system continues to offer advice on how to correct my course, suggesting places for me to make U-turns and ways to get back on track to the original way that I was going. At this point, I turn the system off so as not to be pestered by its intermittent interfering.

Unfortunately, my sense of direction is not always as keen as I think it is and as a consequence, I find myself lost and unable to make it to my destination. I then grudgingly turn my system back on knowing that it will start advising me once more. And when I do, it always begins with these words, "the system is re-routing." Isn't that wonderful? I am not forced to listen to a lecture of how I never should have veered off or that I should have listened when opportunities were given to me to turn around. Instead, I get the "re-routing" prompt followed quickly by a new course to take me to my destination.

This is what God does for us when He calls us to repent. No lectures – just the glad re-routing of our lives back into right relationship with Him. Jesus summarized his entire ministry with one sentence - "Repent for the Kingdom of God is at hand" Repent literally means turn to a new direction. The Kingdom refers to new life in Christ, and at hand means that it is available to all right now. Jesus' call for all of humanity to repent was crystallized in his prayer for Simon Peter. In telling him that the focus of his prayer was for Peter to turn back, Jesus was saying that he was offering a path back from the place of rebellion. As we pray for repentance, God provides us with a free path back to Him. Any price we pay is not exacted by Him, but by life which always taxes those who disobey and disregard God's word and way.

God's freely given gift of repentance should not be taken for granted. It is a call of urgency – the Kingdom of God is at hand. So many people have ended up broken, stranded, out of gas, or out of time because they have chosen to go their own route rather than the one that God is directing them to. It is not that God was unwilling to re-route them, but that they were unable to cover the distance of their destiny. Prayer is the voice of God navigating us toward abundant life. It is bad to choose our own path. It is even worse to shut off His voice for then we truly become lost.

Reflection Question

Can you recall a time when you got off track, refused to listen to God's voice and ended up lost from your destination?

#ignite50Day40

DAY 41 | Not Disowned or Disinherited

Hebrews 10:1-10
Key Verse: 10

By that will we have been sanctified through
the offering of the body of Jesus Christ once for all.

When I recall the ways in which I rebelled against my parents' love and leadership during my teenage years, I am motivated to call them and apologize again some twenty-five years later. As I grew into what I thought at the time was manhood, I would storm away from my parents, usually my father, full of self-created righteous indignation and anger. Later on, after I cooled down and realized that I was in the wrong, I would slink back to my father usually without ever formally acknowledging my wrong. Yet, he would not hold it over my head or make me feel worse. Even though he would have been well within his rights to disown me, instead he loved me and gathered me back into his embrace.

In court, confession of guilt often does not result in dispensation of punishment. A guilty plea often may be met with release, with time served, a suspended sentence, or simply a warning, or an opportunity to have the accused's record expunged. Even our legal system recognizes the need to provide a path towards redemption and rehabilitation. Likewise, God's declaration is always one that restores and redeems the fallen.

This is the mystery of Jesus' sacrifice on the Cross at Calvary. While the law demanded our disqualification from fellowship with God, the atoning blood of Jesus literally accepts our guilty sentence and punishment and it offers us new life instead. The writer of Hebrews underscores the significance of the blood of Jesus by showing us that it did what no animal sacrifice could do. It cleansed once and for all. When this revelation is internalized, it begins to shift our prayer life from a dull routine to a sincere and amazing opportunity to be renewed by the same sacrificial love.

When we pray from a place of being loved, freely acknowledging that we have willfully turned away from God, we are amazed that God has graciously chosen not to reward us according to our sin. This should cause anyone with a conscience to be overwhelmed with a flood of gratitude and appreciation. It ignites the soul with a hunger and thirst to be united with the one who bore our sins.

It is here that prayer comes alive and breathes on its own. This is when our minds rush to catch up with the Holy Spirit who shares mysteries that are too wonderful for us to grasp. It is when our hearts beat with the overwhelming sense of God's presence and compassion. There is a place of ecstasy and delight in prayer that fulfills our soul's yearning for safety and solace. All of our vain efforts in life are only attempts to manufacture what God has freely given to us in prayer.

Reflection Question

Does the revelation of Jesus' sacrifice spiritually ignite you?

Chapter Seven:
PRAYER OF PURPOSE AND ASSIGNMENT

"strengthen your brothers."

DAY 42 | FOLLOWING THROUGH ON PRAYER

LUKE 22:31-32
Key Verse: 32
"Strengthen your brothers"

Real football fans are familiar with one of the most valuable and overlooked tactics involved in every game. It involves the instances where someone is running with the ball. Early on players are trained to fall forward. This training presupposes that most plays will not end with the player running untouched into the end zone. Therefore, since the play will end up in a tackle- the key is to get as much as possible out of the play that fails to reach its ultimate goal. As a consequence, the act of falling forward increases forward progress, and makes more possible the ability to score and win the game.

As believers we must recognize that we fall short of our expectations and God's. The key in these times is to gain as much from our falls as possible so that ultimately we may advance our cause - the Kingdom of God. One of the greatest things that you can know is that you have not disqualified yourself from God's plan. In fact, if you have doubted, resisted, or flatly refused to consent to God's purpose for your life, you stand in good company. The Bible is replete with individuals who failed and fell forward. Whether Moses, who referenced his speech impediment, Gideon who considered himself to weak, Jonah boarding a boat to escape his assignment or Esther who did not want to fall out of favor with the king, or even Jesus who flatly requested to know whether there was another means to achieve the salvation of humanity, in each instance, those who initially resisted their role, found that this was not a disqualifying act.

When Jesus warns Simon Peter of his faith fall (after you have turned back strengthen your brothers), he also informs him that his fall does not eliminate God's assignment for his life. In fact, it appears that his fall will aid in his assisting others who have fallen. To be convicted of falling short is a part of the Christian experience, but praying about our failures and falls allows us to make forward progress. Through sincere prayerful acknowledgment of our shortcomings, God's conviction is re-cycled into conversion. In this moment of transformation our cause and the cause of Christ are advanced.

Reflection Question

How has God revealed your times of falling short as a way to still move forward for the advancement of His kingdom? In other words, how has God taken what seems like shortcomings as steps toward fulfilling His plan and purpose for your life?

#ignite50Day42

DAY 43 | LET PRAYER GUIDE YOUR MISSION STATEMENT

LUKE 4:16-19
Key Verse: 18
"The Spirit of the Lord is upon me"

Most successful organizations have a clear mission statement that defines who they are, and what they are called to do which ultimately becomes the guiding principle. Jesus began his ministry with this same kind of mission statement. When Simon first received his new name, he was given information about his office, but not about how to fulfill its assignment. To say that he would serve as the rock of the church did not speak to how to serve in that capacity. Here Jesus makes plain not simply demonic attack, but his divine assignment. After the devil has done his worse, and Peter's faith survives – God then wants Peter to strengthen his brothers, which is the church.

For years football teams have studied the "film" of their past games. The point is to analyze mistakes and identify opportunities to improve their individual play which will enhance the teams' overall performance. While players have a role in this process, it is really the coach who is expected to make the key findings and determine what play will benefit the team overall. The Holy Spirit is our coach, convicting us when we play poorly, and leading and guiding us into all truth. Our challenge is to learn the lessons that the coach desires to share with us so that mistakes of our past do not become the scripts of our future.

Our lives of prayer not only reveal what we're supposed to do, but how we're supposed to do it. While there are so many books that can help us to discover our purpose, only prayer can tell us how to fulfill that purpose. Prayer will reveal to you suitable mentors and co-laborers, the proper track of preparation and opportunities that God has ordained. Just as importantly, God can reveal to us through prayer, the betrayals, and disappointments that have also served in preparation for the strength that we need for our faith to survive and to help our brothers and sisters in Christ.

Reflection Question

In what ways can you use your survival through trying times as a way to help strengthen your church?

DAY 44 | YOUR FALL EMPOWERS YOU TO EMPOWER OTHERS

ROMANS 8:28-30
Key Verse: 28
And we know that all things work together
for good to those who love God, to those who
are the called according to His purpose.

A story is told of a man who unwittingly fell into an open manhole while crossing the street. Injured and unable to crawl his way out the hole, he called out for help. A doctor passed by and when the man indicated that he had hurt himself, the doctor encouraged the man to see him when he got out so that he could set the man's leg. He dropped his card in the hole and kept going. A lawyer came along, heard him, and dropped his card into the hole, and encouraged the man to call so that they could sue the city. Finally, the man's' friend happened by, recognized his voice and jumped in the hole. The man became discouraged saying, "what were you thinking, you should have gotten a rope or a ladder. Now you're trapped as well." The friend replied, "don't worry about it, I've been down here before and I know the way out."

What often allows us the ability to assist others in their struggles is that we have been where they are and we know the way out. This kind of personal ministry is not from doctor to patient, but from patient to patient with one person a few steps further along in recovery than the other. This is Simon Peter's assignment as articulated by Jesus. Once he has been restored, Peter is to go back and help to restore his brothers in the faith. When ministry is offered from a place of empathy born from one's experience, it is both authentic and effective.

Ultimately, Jesus' prayer for Simon Peter was that he would recover from his fall, and based on this experience, go back and assist the others with their recovery. One of the mysteries of our walk with the Lord is how our worst moments can lead to our finest hours. Foundational to a vibrant prayer life is a belief in this mystery that somehow God can bring order out of chaos. We must pray trusting in the declaration that Paul makes in Romans 8:28, *"we know that all things work together for good for those who love God, who are called according to his purpose."* We must have confidence that God can reconfigure our experiences and channel them towards our eventual benefit and His ultimate glory.

Jesus' prayer for Simon Peter was precisely that what Satan would attempt would ultimately work to the advantage of the disciples and the church. Of course, God takes no glory from evil, and we should never attempt to tie personal tragedies to God. Yet, out of the ashes of life, greater strength of faith and testimonies are born. Survivors of abuse, abandonment, adultery and addiction are able to take from the ashes of their most painful moments in life, the truths, lessons, and testimonies that can assist others. When prayers for relief and release from troubles and trials in life seemingly go unanswered, it may be time to pray not simply to survive what we are facing, but to allow our survival to point someone else to Christ.

Reflection Question

In what ways have your own struggles helped others who have similar struggles to yours?

DAY 45 | PRAYER IS YOUR MEANS OF COMMUNICATING TO GOD

2 KINGS 20: 1-7

Key Verse: 2-3

Then he turned his face toward the wall, and prayed to the LORD, saying, ³"Remember now, O LORD, I pray, how I have walked before You in truth and with a loyal heart, and have done what was good in Your sight." And Hezekiah wept bitterly.

When members of the armed services are deployed on the battlefield, they are usually outfitted with communication equipment. It is understood that in order to coordinate their efforts with the rest of the unit, it is necessary to talk to one another. The presumption is that the equipment will not be used for idle chatter or individual concerns, but will be used to accomplish the mission of the group.

Unfortunately, most of our communication with God falls in the category of idle chatter or is consumed with individual concerns. At some point, though, we ought to exercise the power of prayer to focus on the mission of the unit – which in this case is the Kingdom of God. God is concerned for each of us and it is His good pleasure to bless us. If we take into consideration that our blessings are already assured, then it is only appropriate to spend our prayerful attention and energy focusing on God's callings and assignments for our lives.

These assignments may include serving as a surrogate parent or mentor to a young person in our community who does not have a positive example of Christian faith. Our assignment may be undergirding a ministry with our time, talents or treasure. Whatever we are called to do, we ought to treat it as so vital and significant that we become inseparable from the calling. When we do so, we open a new channel of effective prayer.

In this passage, God has just told Hezekiah, through the prophet Isaiah, to set his house in order because he was unable to recover from the sickness that caused him great suffering. Hezekiah's response was to turn his face to the wall and pray to God. He then spoke to the Lord about his service and faithfulness to Him. It is important to note that Hezekiah is not speaking to God from a place of entitlement as if God owes him a favor; rather, he speaks as one who has made himself open to be used by God, who will no longer be available for service.

At this point in the prayer, God speaks to Isaiah and tells him to return to Hezekiah and inform him that He has changed His mind and that Hezekiah will be given fifteen more years.

Whenever we are able to move our prayers beyond ourselves and to our Kingdom purposes, we offer God more space to move on our behalf. Rather than seeking money for material enjoyment, when we have a heart to sow into missions, we open a new channel in prayer. When we seek to develop our leadership abilities or advance our skill sets to strengthen the ministries of our church, we open a new channel.

My favorite hymn, "Draw Me Nearer," has a verse that says: "Consecrate me now to thy service Lord by the power of divine grace. Let my soul look up with a steadfast hope and my will be lost in thine." Whenever we pray in the spirit of this hymn, we open a new channel.

Reflection Question

In what way do you sense God leading you through prayer to open a new channel?

DAY 46 | MY SURVIVAL SAVES SOMEONE ELSE'S LIFE

JAMES 4:6
God resists the proud, But gives grace to the humble.

My favorite part of pre-flight instructions is when the flight attendant is referring to the use of oxygen masks in the event that the cabin of the plane loses pressure. It goes as follows: *If you are traveling with someone who needs assistance, put on your mask first, then offer assistance.* The message could not be any clearer. You can only help others once you have helped yourself. It is important to remember that God does not save us, bless us, or deliver us just for us. God does so with the expectation that after we have been helped we will offer assistance to someone else. In fact, God desires that we extend the grace that we have received, to someone else.

Prayer helps us as wounded healers. Before we are able to minister to others we must be ministered to by others and by God through prayer. Self-help in the Kingdom of God begins with the admission that you cannot help yourself. When you make this confession of inadequacy you assume the proper posture of humility which makes your heart accessible to be transformed by the power of prayer.

James 4:6 declares "*God resists the proud, but gives grace to the humble.*" Now God has you right where God wants you. First, you will be better by being broken in this way because you will mend and be stronger than you first began. Secondly, your brokenness will allow you to see others' brokenness with more grace than judgment. Finally, your grace-aided perspective will allow you to aid in restoring their brokenness.

As I've gotten older, I've endured a number of athletic injuries that have required the attention of a physical therapist as a part of my recovery. It is clear that their work is informed not simply from physiological theory. Their ability to push me to the limit without re-injuring me is a result of their training when they are put in the position of the patient, so that they can feel and know what is happening. Of course, when a trainer shares their experience of having had the same or a similar injury, this is most helpful because it adds an extra sense of credibility. They know personally how it feels, and they are living proof that the therapy works. It is important to understand that we cannot claim some unique place of suffering to which we cannot relate. Whenever we have overcome great personal and spiritual challenges, not only do we have a testimony to give out of the experience, but also an intuitive sensitivity to how to minister to those with similar needs as ours.

A very critical part of being transformed by Christ for Christ is to realize that ministry is about being relatable. We must learn to use our experiences, good and bad, to show others about the transformative and life-changing power of Jesus Christ.

Reflection Question

How transformative do you feel that your prayer life has been through this seven-week devotional study? How will you continue igniting your prayer life?

DAY 47 | I ALONE AM LEFT — THE DANGER OF SINGLING YOURSELF OUT

1KINGS 19:11-18

Key Verse: 14

And he said, "I have been very zealous for the LORD God of hosts; because the children of Israel have forsaken Your covenant, torn down Your altars, and killed Your prophets with the sword. I alone am left; and they seek to take my life."

It has been my experience that as church folks, both ministers and members, we have the habit of thinking of ourselves as being nobler than others. Whenever we think of ourselves as having a purer love for God, or having suffered more than others, we become awash in a strange sense of entitlement. If left unchecked, this self-centered perspective draws us into a place of self-righteousness and draws us away from God. This was the case of Elijah, who after defeating the priests of Baal on Mt. Carmel, finds himself running away from the threats of Jezebel while at the same time feeling very sorry for himself.

In an outburst of emotion, Elijah compares himself to the rest of the Israelite nation characterizing himself as more zealous for the Lord and then listing the blasphemous actions of others. He concludes his complaint by declaring, "I alone am left, and now they (Jezebel and Ahab) are seeking to take my life. The '*I alone*' syndrome is commonly heard amongst the saints who believe their motivation in giving is to be seen as more pure, their work in ministry to have come by greater sacrifice, and even their worship to be more sincere.

One of the blessings of prayer is that it puts the '*I alone*' sentiment in check. Prayer allows God to speak and provides for us His perspective on how noble we really are. God answered Elijah by giving him a list of individuals to be anointed to serve in kingly and priestly and prophetic roles. Then God reminded Elijah that he is not alone, but in fact that God had seven thousand other people who had not bowed their knees to Baal.

As a teenager, I remember complaining to a friend about how unfair it was that I had to sing in the choir, serve as an usher, and work in the media ministry. My friend began to rub his thumb and index finger together while wearing a wide smile. When I asked him what he was doing he replied, "I'm playing the world's smallest violin to accompany your sob story." Now we both were laughing out loud, as I had failed to recognize that he was in all of the same ministries but did not have the same attitude that I did. He was a good friend for moving me past my 'I alone' perspective. God becomes that same friend through prayer.

Reflection Question

In what specific areas do you need God's help in ridding yourself of the 'I alone' syndrome?

#ignite50Day47

117

DAY 48 | PRAYING WITH PASSION FOR YOUR PURPOSE

JONAH 1:1-6

Key Verse: 3

But Jonah arose to flee to Tarshish from the presence of the LORD. He went down to Joppa, and found a ship going to Tarshish; so he paid the fare, and went down into it, to go with them to Tarshish from the presence of the LORD.

It is important to distinguish between our passions and our purpose. Unfortunately there is an abundance of self-help theory, New Age religion, and even popular Christian teaching that use these words interchangeably. Obviously we can be passionate about our purpose, but it is no guarantee that this is how it will work out for us. Jonah's purpose could not have been any clearer. God told him explicitly to go and preach repentance to the Ninevites. Jonah's problem was that he deeply hated the Ninevites and would have preferred to see them destroyed in judgment than spared the wrath of God through repentance. The notion that he would aid in their deliverance was too much for him to handle as it was opposite of his hateful passion. And with his passion out of odds with his purpose, he followed his passion, paid his fare, and boarded a boat to literally go away from his Godly purpose.

Our prayer life is vital to fulfilling our purpose because it compensates for our lack of passion in areas of purpose. Nowhere does the Bible say that Jonah wrestled in prayer with God about his offense at God's assignment for his life. Nowhere does Jonah consider the fact that he himself has been a recipient of the same grace that God is calling him to share with the Ninevites. It is only after the storm, in the belly of a fish, that Jonah is ready to put purpose above passion.

Instead of needing calamity to convince us that God's purpose is better than our passion, an active prayer life puts things in proper perspective and empowers us to serve in roles for which we have little to no passion. When your purpose is attending to an aged parent, it's difficult to be passionate about some of the sacrifices, and indelicate moments that this purpose requires. When your purpose is to bring reconciliation in your family by modeling forgiveness and long suffering, you'll need prayer to compensate for passion. Prayer relieves us of negative tensions, and enlivens us to carry out our purpose with excellence.

The Lord's expectation of us when we are dispassionate is to substitute our reticence or loathing for the task or goal with our abounding passion for Him. Paul begins his powerful letter to the church in Rome by referring to himself as a slave of Christ. Let this image sink in. Paul never thought of life in Christ as being a means by which one fulfills his dreams, or pursues their own interests. Rather Paul understood the new life in Christ to be a life of slavery- where one submits to the will of the master, and dutifully attends to every assignment and order that one is given. This image is the perfect picture of Jesus' delineation of discipleship. In essence Jesus is saying, "If you want to be my disciple let him deny himself -his passions, his dreams, and desires to take up his cross, accept the burdens and challenges of this new life. And follow me, modify both your path and your walk, to be like mine." Only through prayer can the Holy Spirit move us from self-centered beings toward becoming slaves of Christ.

Reflection Question

What are you passionate about and how can your passion help to make you a more fruitful disciple for Jesus Christ?

#ignite50Day48

DAY 49 | AND PETER

MARK 16:1-8

Key Verse: 8

But go, tell His disciples—and Peter—that He is going before you into Galilee; there you will see Him, as He said to you.

In between Jesus' resurrection on Easter and the manifestation of the Holy Spirit on Pentecost Sunday, Jesus appears to teach and share. While these messages were challenging and life-changing for all who heard them, Peter must have taken from them something more. The resurrected Jesus helped to put all of the pieces of the puzzle in place for Peter. He now understood why Jesus referred to the need to be crucified. It now made sense that someone had to be designated as the rock of the church, just as it now became clear why Satan had specifically targeted Peter, and why Jesus had prayed for him.

Like a soldier who has experienced the horrors of the battlefield for the first time who listens with new intensity at his next training, so Peter now must recognize why he must seek to model in substance and style the ministry of the Master. I am fond of saying that "experience is not the best teacher because her tuition is too high." While the pains and mistakes of our experience may prove instructive, thankfully they are not the sole means of our understanding of God's will for our lives. God speaks by His word and by His spirit. Thus, a prayer life rooted in the word of God helps us to understand our role in the kingdom.

Of course this begs the question, what about our prayer life is Kingdom-focused? If we simply pray about the personal and practical challenges of life, we miss the real goal of being saved. While God is both interested and involved in the daily affairs of humanity, He is most concerned with the expansion of His Kingdom on earth as it is in heaven. Peter's Kingdom-focus is brought into view through what Jesus has told him, and how the circumstances of his life have unfolded. Can there be any real doubt that Peter must have spent the fifty days between Easter and Pentecost in intense prayer? Certainly, the Peter that emerges on Pentecost is not the same one that had deserted Jesus on Good Friday.

This is why the angel instructed the women at the tomb of Jesus to tell the disciples, *and Peter*. The fact that he was singled out was yet another indication of his special role and responsibility. When we spend time in prayer, God is able to reveal the specific and detailed kingdom role that has been assigned to our lives.

Reflection Question

How can you help others be more kingdom-focused in their prayer life?

DAY 50 | LET THIS BE KNOWN TO YOU

ACTS 2: 1-47

Key Verse: 14

But Peter, standing up with the eleven, raised his voice and said to them, "Men of Judea and all who dwell in Jerusalem, let this be known to you, and heed my words.

The plant that sprouts from the ground has undergone a long and difficult process just to achieve its arrival in a new world. The warmth of the sun, the nourishment of water and nutrients of the soil, and the stubbornness of rocks have each played a part in helping or hindering the sapling as it struggled in this unseen place beneath the surface of the earth.

Its appearance represents a huge victory born of great struggle and effort, and the beginning of a whole new struggle in a brand new environment much like Peter on the day of Pentecost. After the Holy Spirit fell and believers began to speak in other tongues, Peter rebukes the naysayers who accused the believers of being drunkards. In this moment he also preaches a sermon that leads to 3,000 people converting their lives to be followers of Christ. In this instance, Peter is that young sapling. His bold entry into this new world is the result of a long invisible struggle of faith that occurred over the prior fifty days.

From the moment of Jesus' resurrection, Peter's progress in faith was central in the mind of God. Peter's influence over the others is obvious in that even after Jesus' first week post-resurrection wherein he revealed himself twice to the disciples in the locked house, Peter ended up leading the others not in witnessing but in fishing.

This was more than a recreational or vocational venture. It was a sign spiritually that Peter intended to return to his pre-Jesus way of life. But when Jesus appears on the shore and John reveals his identity, Peter leads the charge for the men to return back to Jesus. While the others were content to wait on the boat, Peter leaps into the water to swim back to the Savior.

Over the next forty-two days Jesus reveals himself to his disciples, teaching them and showing them more signs and wonders. None of the Gospel writers give us a view into Peter's personal development. It happens beneath the surface. Based on his history, there are certain things that we can be almost certain of when it comes to Peter. He interjected his opinion on the spiritual matters that were unfolding as he did on the Mountain of Transfiguration (Matthew 17: 1-13). Certainly, Peter jumped to a wrong conclusion or two as he did when he rebuked Jesus for speaking about his Crucifixion. And certainly Peter prayed as he did for Jesus in the Garden of Gethsemane (hopefully without falling asleep this time).

Peter must have taken to heart all the things that Jesus shared with him and he must have prayed over them. It probably is just as well that we don't see or hear his prayer during his fifty-day journey. After all, we are admonished not to pray out loud like hypocrites, but to go into our secret prayer closets (Matthew 6:5). We cannot know how many times Peter prayed because the scriptures do not reveal that to us. But the results of his prayers are obvious. It is both Peter's prayer life during the days leading up to Pentecost, as well as Jesus' prayer for Peter that he would turn back to him after betraying the Savior, that have served as the basis of this book.

On the day of Pentecost, Peter stands and fulfills the promise of Jesus' prayer. Peter turns back and strengthens his brothers. He has become what Jesus had in mind when he first changed the disciple's name from Simon to Peter. Jesus' prayer has been fulfilled in that Satan's attempts at sifting him had not been successful. Peter and the disciples fell away briefly, but Peter's faith did not fail.

Jesus' prayer has proven triumphant as the Holy Spirit falls like cloven tongues of fire to ignite the life of the church. The prayer life of Jesus ignited the life of the church back then in Acts 2 and it ignites our prayer life even now. I know by the power of the Holy Spirit that you have also experienced fifty days of prayer that have changed your life.

ABOUT THE AUTHOR

The Reverend Matthew L. Watley is the Executive Minister of Reid Temple AME Church where he founded the church's North Campus in Silver Spring, MD in 2006. The Lord has blessed this ministry by growing the congregation from 200 to more than 4000. Rev. Watley holds a BA and M.Div. from Howard University, a Master's Degree in Executive Leadership from Georgetown University, and he is currently pursuing the Executive Doctorate in Leadership at The George Washington University. He is married to the former Shawna Francis, and they are the proud parents of Alexandra Elizabeth. Throughout his career, Rev. Watley has received numerous academic, civic, literary, and ecclesiastical awards. Concerning these and other accomplishments, he submits that, "The challenge of servant-leadership is not to win acclaim or to amass honor, but to do justice, to love mercy, and to walk humbly with God." Micah 6:8

CONTACT:
twitter: @matthewwatley
web: www.matthewwatley.com